ALL ACCESS
COMIN' TO YOUR CITY
2006
250

Big & Rich

ALL ACCESS

Big & Rich
ALL ACCESS

Big Kenny & John Rich

WITH ALLEN RUCKER

CENTER STREET

New York Boston Nashville

Center Street
Hachette Book Group USA
237 Park Avenue
New York, NY 10017

Visit our Web site at www.centerstreet.com

Center Street is a division of Hachette Book Group USA.
The Center Street name and logo are trademarks of Hachette Book Group USA.
Printed in the United States of America

First Edition: June 2007

10 9 8 7 6 5 4 3 2 1

Library of Congress Cataloging-in-Publication Data
Rich, John, 1974–
Big & Rich : all access / Big Kenny and John Rich ;
with Allen Rucker. — 1st ed.
p. cm.
Summary: The fully authorized, uninhibited, entirely true story
of how Big & Rich are taking over country music.
ISBN-13: 978-1-59995-717-3
ISBN-10: 1-59995-717-5
1. Big & Rich.   2. Country musicians—United States—Biography.
I. Big Kenny, 1963–   II. Rucker, Allen.   III. Title.
IV. Title: Big and Rich.
ML421.B53R53 2007
782.421642092'2—dc22
[B]
2006101320

BROTHERS & SISTERS . . .

FRIENDS, FAMILY & FANS, SO MANY
WONDERFUL THINGS HAVE HAPPENED IN
OUR LIVES OVER THE PAST FEW YEARS
AS THE WORLD OF "BIG & RICH" HAS GROWN.

OUR HEARTFELT THANKS GOES
OUT TO EACH AND EVERY ONE OF
YOU FOR BEING THE MOST IMPORTANT
PART OF MAKING OUR DREAMS COME
TRUE. YOU ALL ARE THE REASON
WE DO WHAT WE DO AND WITH YOUR
CONTINUED SUPPORT & ENCOURAGEMENT
THE FUTURE SURE IS BRIGHT FOR US ALL!
WE LOVE YOU,

CONTENTS

ACKNOWLEDGMENTS

Books like these don't write themselves. It is with our deepest gratitude that we thank our co-writer Allen Rucker. His patience and perception truly took our crazy story and molded it into something that makes sense.

Books don't design, edit, and publish themselves either. To our friends at Hachette books, our publisher Rolf, our editor Christina, and our design and production team, our deepest gratitude. What a pleasure it has been going through this process of self evaluation with you.

What a wonderful team we have. A special thanks to our literary agent Mel Berger, our personal agent Greg Oswald, our legal eagle Jess Rosen, our accountant Dwight Wiles, and our managers Marc Oswald and Dale Morris.

The gang in the office and on the road: Sheila Hozhabri for coordinating the whole book, our tour manager Shawn Pennington, the band, and the crew.

To the many directors and producers who have helped to capture our image: our boy Chappy who wrote, produced, and directed the "8th of November" long form documentary, our photographers Joe Hardwick and Kristin Barlow, Jeff Richter, David Hogan, and the Deaton Flanigen boys who produced and directed most of our videos including, "Save a Horse," "Holy Water," "Big Time," and the epic "8th of November."

Everybody at Warner Bros. records, beginning with Espo, Paul, Bill, Dirmuid, Tom, Jules, Peter, Lynette, Gator, Jimmy, and the rest of the team.

To the Alphin & Rich Families: Thank you for your constant support. Kenny would especially like to thank his wife Christiev for the love that keeps him alive, his son Lincoln for more inspiration than he could ever have imagined, and his mom, Mary.

To the Muzik Mafia: Gretchen, King Jon, Cory, and the rest of the family. What can we say? We were the little train that could, and we did.

To our friends at Country Radio, the greatest format on earth, CMT, GAC, and *Country Weekly*. Thank you for allowing the Big & Rich love train to roll down your airwaves and across your pages.

It is all of your combined efforts that enabled the Big & Rich dream to come true. For those of you who we may have forgotten to mention, our most sincere apology. It is with a humble heart that we express our gratitude to each of you.

Finally, to our dear friends Katie Darnell and Master Sergeant Niles Harris, your stories have inspired us to think beyond ourselves and our self interests.

And don't forget . . . VOTE RICH IN 2024.

COUNTRY MUSIC WITHOUT PREJUDICE

WELCOME

" . . . Brothers and sisters
We are here for one reason
And one reason alone
To share our love of muzikaaaahhhh."

That's the position we staked out in the very first words of our very first album, and by God, we're sticking to it.

Hello, I'm Big Kenny,
and I'm John Rich,
and this is our book.

That's nice, but who are we, really? Well, we're two incredibly lucky guys who teamed up as Big & Rich in 2003 to create the kind of music both of us had been working on our whole lives. We are not your average country music duo, if there is such a thing, and in fact some people don't think of us as country artists at all. Nevertheless, we've sold a few records, sold out a few concerts, and probably aren't going to go away for a while. Not if the Freak Parade has anything to do with it.

The Freak Parade is the name we've given to our fans—you know who you are—and they are a crazy, diverse, and rowdy bunch. This book is first and foremost for them, or you. In the same way that we love to share our love of music, we thought it might be a good idea to concoct a kind of Big & Rich family album, full of stories and photos of our life both on and off the road.

"Somebody's got to be unafraid to lead the Freak Parade."

We've only been an official twosome for four years or so (as we're writing this book), and have only been performing in concert for four years, but we've stored up a lifetime of memories. In that relatively short span of time, it's already been a long, strange, and joyous trip. We've traveled all over the world; found a spiritual home in Deadwood, South Dakota; spent two hundred or more days a year on the road doing concerts and benefits; appeared on TV and talked on radio; and still carved out the time to carry on with all our friends in our Nashville circle of fellow musicians and misfits known as the Muzik Mafia.

We love what we do and we are having a seriously good time doing it. We hope you have an equally good time flipping through this book and learning a little about where we've been on this magical musical journey, and about some of the incredible people we've met up with along the way.

Step off the curb, friend, and join the Freak Parade.

WHAT IS COUNTRY MUSIC?

When we started out, we were thrown that question constantly, almost as much as the standard ones about where Big Kenny got his top hat or why John dressed so much flashier than Big Kenny.

Needless to say, this thinking drove us nuts. Both of our musical identities are deeply and firmly rooted in the history of country music. Our main influences, especially lyrically, are the great singer-songwriters of the country tradition. We are, in every way, as country as cheese grits and stock car racing. We just happen to define *country* in a broader and more inclusive way, that's all.

As John puts it, **"We're both country boys, but could not be from more different parts of the country. However, we're connected on that musical level that I'm the only guy he knows like me and he's the only guy I know like him. And when you've got something like that, I don't think you would ever really be able to break it."**

"Country music without prejudice."

We call it "country muzik without prejudice." That means a lot of things. First of all, it means music without the restrictions of artificial or market-driven boundaries. It also means music without prejudice against someone's skin color or birthplace or musical entry point. They haven't kicked Keith Urban out of country because he's from Australia and writes rock-hard country songs. And they once gave Gretchen Wilson a hard time because she was "too" country—that is, a redneck woman who wasn't afraid to say so.

You can't let other people define you or your music, and we are not about to fall into that trap. We've gone too far to turn back now.

This is nothing new, the idea of defining country music in an artistic, rather than commercial, way. Johnny Cash, for instance, one of

John Rich proudly displays this photo of him and Johnny Cash in his home.

Shawn Pennington, Marc Oswald, Big Kenny, and Steve Schweidel pose in front of the Capitol Building.

our true heroes, is now considered the standard for country music. In the general public's mind, there is no one more "country" than the Man in Black. Well, when Johnny pulled into Nashville in 1955, he was considered a rock act. He recorded on Sun Records in Memphis, the studio that brought you Elvis, Jerry Lee Lewis, Howling Wolf, and even Ike Turner of "Ike and Tina" fame. To every true-blue *Grand Ole Opry* listener and country fan at the time, that wasn't "country"! That was rockabilly, or rhythm and blues, or, God forbid, rock and roll.

When he showed up in Music City, Johnny Cash didn't have a fiddle player or a steel guitar, and he wasn't wearing a string tie or rhinestone suits. He dressed like an undertaker and sang songs with a driving, almost hypnotic beat about sex and violence: "I shot a man in Reno / Just to watch him die." Probably a lot of people in Nashville at the time saw him coming and said, "Well, if that down-and-dirty rockabilly stuff is country music, I'm leaving the business."

They didn't leave, of course, they just adjusted. They adjusted to Johnny, then to Kris Kristofferson, Willie Nelson, Waylon Jennings, Merle Haggard, Hank Jr., Alabama, and a hundred other mavericks who strolled into town and expanded the music in a hundred new directions. Today Willie Nelson, as country as they come, is as much a country jazz artist as anything else. If you think back, Patsy Cline, another country revolutionary, is kind of a country version of a great blues singer like Ella Fitzgerald. They are distinct and original. That's why country music opened up to include them.

A lot of people who don't listen to country music, and look down on it as hokey and tradition-bound, still think of the whole genre as polyester suits and gingham dresses, dum-diddy-dum rhythms, and cornball lyrics about the folks back in Hicksville. Then you ask them, "You don't care much for country music, but do you like Johnny Cash?"

"Oh, yeah, I love Johnny Cash!"

"What about Dwight Yoakam? Do you like him?"

"Oh, he's great. He's so sexy!"

"Or what about Willie Nelson singing 'Stardust,' a Tin Pan Alley song written by Hoagy Carmichael in 1927 and recorded by Louis Armstrong and Frank Sinatra?"

"Oh, that's a classic. I play that song every day."

The point is, it's *all* country music—it's all music rooted in the uniquely American style that is also the basis of the country tradition—and the category of "country" will only get bigger and more varied, not less so. Big Kenny has another term he likes to throw around: *creativity without bureaucracy*. The demands of marketing, or radio formats, or simply "the way we've always done it," should in no way dictate what songwriters and singers want to say musically. Whatever you create in your head, you should try to realize to the fullest extent, not fit into some preordained box.

Or at least, that's how we see it, and it's kind of worked for us so far.

ALL ACCESS

So, having gotten that question out of the way (and there will be a pop quiz after you finish the book), it's time to move on. Consider this a look at the world from the other side of the stage, from our point of view, us looking out at you and not vice versa.

Imagine this:

You're at one of the informal after-concert jam sessions we like to have, usually at a local bar where the only announcement is by word of mouth and pretty soon a thousand or more people have shown up and are trying to fit in a barroom made for seventy-five. Anyway, you bribe the bouncer and get in, meet us, and we hit it off, becoming old friends in an instant—the way it sometimes happens. We have such a good time kicking back together, we invite you to come along to our next tour stop.

Shawn Pennington, our tour manager, gives you a laminated pass to hang around your neck with the words ALL ACCESS in big letters. That means you are permitted to go anywhere on or off the stage you want—the dressing rooms, the backstage hangout room (or "green room"), all the tech areas, and even the buses we ride around in.

This book is in fact an all-access pass into our lives, before, during, and after a big concert. We're bringing you inside the Big Top and backstage to see who we are, how we got to where we are, and where we plan to go from here.

Since we're at the beginning of our tour, let's first head backstage—into the lives of Big

Kenny and John Rich long before we were Big & Rich, and how we got to this once-in-a-lifetime collision of two distinct musical planets. **"One of the things I think is important in this book is to get across how drastically different John and I are. We're just different characters, man, yet we meet together every night on that stage and play our music,"** Kenny says.

Then we'll invite you to a Tuesday-night get-together at the Pub of Luv in Nashville to meet the Muzik Mafia—the band of merry musicians and oddball artists who provided the love, support, and insanity that finally led to the birth of Big & Rich.

Next, we'll drag you into the studio for the making of our first album, *Horse of a Different Color,* a set of songs that had some people in country scratching their heads and others embracing us, showing up at our concerts, and buying our CD. We just knew in our gut that there were "a few hundred million more like me / just trying to keep it free," to quote the song "Rollin' (The Ballad of Big & Rich)"—and hey, we were right! We will take you backstage to feel the exhilaration of going from nobodies to somebodies, including the day we made the most outrageous video we'd ever seen, let alone created—the one for "Save a Horse (Ride a Cowboy)."

We'll go on the road with Cowboy Troy, Two Foot Fred, Adam the Atomic guitar player, and the rest of the Big & Rich revue, introducing you to the

Filming the "Save a Horse (Ride a Cowboy)" video.

Freak Parade of incredible, fanatical, and, perhaps in some cases, mentally questionable fans who make this the greatest damn job on earth. Pay attention. That might be your fan letter we're quoting or your local honky-tonk where we decided to pull out our acoustic guitars and play whatever we please.

It was on the road, very early on, where we met a guy with a long gray ponytail named Niles Harris in a bar in Deadwood, South Dakota, and heard his story of heroism and sacrifice in Vietnam in the 1960s. This led to our song and video "8th of November," and our commitment to recognizing the efforts of brave men and women who have served their country in the military, some of whom have long been forgotten. This is one aspect of Big & Rich you might not have known about before you came along on this trip. We are passionate about everything from the human tragedy of Darfur in northern Africa to the human tragedy of spousal

ABOVE TOP: Two Foot Fred and our production manager, Curt Jenkins.

ABOVE: Big Kenny welcomes his son, Lincoln, to the world.

RIGHT: Big & Rich take New York City by storm.

abuse going on next door to a lot of us in America. Big Kenny's constant mantra of LOVE EVERYBODY—written right on the back of his guitar—demands that we all pay attention to these problems and do what we can to expose them.

Finally, the tour buses will pull back into Music City, USA, and we're home. Both of our lives have changed radically since "Save a Horse (Ride a Cowboy)" and all the other great things that have happened to us. John is probably the busiest writer-producer in Nashville, and was

COUNTRY MUSIC WITHOUT PREJUDICE xxi

recently named ASCAP's 2006 Songwriter of the Year for the second year in a row. Big Kenny, a man born with an urge to wander around and see the world, found a beautiful wife, Christiev, and together they made a beautiful baby boy named Lincoln William Holiday Alphin. Come on by the house and meet him. He'll sing you a pirate song.

That's it. The all-purpose, all-encompassing, all-dimensional All Access tour of our lives. We hope you have a good time and if there is anything we left out, please let us know. We'll put it in the next book.

Saddle up and welcome to Music Without Prejudice!

Big & Rich

Big & Rich
ALL ACCESS

WHEN TWO PLANETS COLLIDE

BIG KENNY: "So I guess John was looking for something to do, so he came to my show. He was standing in the back of the room and when the show was over, I had a bag of bubble gum on stage to throw out and I threw one way toward the back and hit him in the head."

JOHN RICH: "It got me right in the face. And I thought, *All right, now I know I really don't like this guy.*"

In the beginning, one of us was essentially a country-tinged rocker and the other was a rock-tinged country singer-songwriter, and we were both struggling to survive in Nashville. We're both country boys, for sure, just country boys from different parts of the country and with slightly different musical personalities, both then and now. From the first time we met to the day we decided to become the entity Big & Rich was a good six years. For that period we just kind of orbited around each other, like two separate musical planets, until we finally collided and merged our two distinct—and unorthodox—styles into one.

The yin and yang.

FROM CULPEPER TO NASHVILLE

Big Kenny comes from an unusually rock-solid family. He was raised on a farm outside Culpeper, Virginia, that's been in his family for eight generations. The farmhouse he grew up in was built before the Revolutionary War, more than 250 years ago. The plumbing is a little better now, but the original house is still standing. His mother, much like her own mother, was born and raised there and still resides there at age seventy-one. It was from his mother that Kenny first developed a love of music—she was the choir director at their church—and the encouragement to live a creative life.

Big Kenny's father, Bill Alphin, is a strong, upstanding man and the closest thing to a saint that Kenny has ever met. At seventy-five, he still raises cattle on the family spread. Although his hip has a way of coming out of joint every so often, he just gets it fixed and keeps on working. He is one tough son of a gun.

Before the day he took off for Nashville, Big Kenny was in construction and helped farm his father's land. His mother urged him to learn to do something with tools. Her thinking was, no matter where you are in life, as long as you have some tools you can be useful and probably employable. To this day, you can sit Big Kenny

BELOW: The Alphin family farm in Culpeper, Virginia.

BELOW RIGHT: Big Kenny clowning around on the family farm, 1981.

in a wood shop or a metal shop and he'll get absolutely lost in making stuff. When you think about it, a craftsman making furniture and a craftsman making music aren't all that different. Just different tools.

Big Kenny sang in church but never had the clichéd country singer's childhood dream to go to Nashville and hit the big time. At twenty-five, he ran a big construction operation in Culpeper, Alphin Homes/Noble Construction, with seventy-five employees and what looked like a lifetime of work. Unfortunately, by the time he hit twenty-nine, there was this thing called the Savings and Loan Scandal. Economic conditions changed overnight, and Big Kenny was completely busted. In one big gust of economic wind, he went from seventy-five employees to one. His real estate holdings were worthless, and he was working nonstop just to fulfill the construction contracts he'd already signed off on.

So one night, Big Kenny was sitting in a bar, nursing his wounds, when someone pushed him on stage to perform with a local musician. He sings a song and sits back down. A few minutes later, the guitar player asks him if he wants to be in a band. Sure, he says, why the hell not? He fondly remembers the band was terrible and he was even worse.

It wasn't long after that when someone told Big Kenny he was a good enough singer and songwriter that he should think about going to Nashville to make a little money.

Big Kenny: "I'm like, what? They actually pay people to write songs? I was so naive that I didn't know songwriting was a paying job. I'd never thought about it."

ABOVE TOP: Big Kenny's Family, 1972. Back row (l to r): Great Aunt Virginia, Goggie, Mom, Dad. Front row (l to r): Ken (aka Big Kenny), Wallace, Rob, Charlene.

ABOVE: Big Kenny and his dad, William Alphin.

If someone had said something about "intellectual property," Big Kenny the farm boy would have been baffled. "Intellectual property? I don't see any damn property. Where's it located?"

In any case, Big Kenny was ready for a change—a big change—so he packed up, locked the door to his house, and "moved to Beverly." It was either a daring move or an insane one, or a little of both.

It took awhile to find his way. Nine years, to be exact. That's how long it was between Big Kenny's arrival in Nashville and the first Big & Rich deal.

FROM AMARILLO TO NASHVILLE

Meanwhile—give or take the ten-year gap in our ages—John was growing up in the high plains of Amarillo, Texas. West Texas has a completely different culture from East Texas or South Texas, let alone Culpeper, Virginia. It's flat and windy out there on the Panhandle, and people have a certain way of doing things, the same way they've been doing things for 150 years or so. The men have leathery, wind-tanned skin, like Clint Eastwood after a long trail ride. They tend to wear ostrich-skin boots (always shined), starched jeans, and some kind of cowboy hat pretty much 365 days a year. They even have rules about hats: No black hats after Memorial Day, and no straw hats after Labor Day. As John likes to say, just look at the hat he's wearing and you'll know what time of year it is.

John as a teen.

Big Kenny tends to put all kinds of things on his head, from top hats to three-colored bandannas, but John pretty much wears a cowboy hat. In West Texas, it's what you would call routine. Out there, some kids ride horses to school and hang their hats on the hat tree found in the corner of every classroom. When the bell rings for the next class, they take their hat and hang it on the next hat tree. And of course you never eat with your hat on. It just isn't done.

At John's school, rodeo was an elective. You could go to class and learn how to rope or cut cows. Both of us were raised around cattle, but in the Amarillo area, there were just a few more head. A cattle ranch in Virginia had two or three hundred animals. A feedlot in West Texas might have two hundred and fifty *thousand* animals at any one time, and if the wind shifts, you can smell that cattle stench a hundred miles away. John claims to like that smell. If an eighteen-wheeler stuffed with cows passes him on the highway, he rolls down the window and takes a big whiff. It reminds him of home. This is how money smelled when he was growing up—not the kind you fold, but the kind that led to food on the table.

John was the oldest of four children, two sisters and a brother. Big Kenny, on the other hand, was the youngest of four siblings, two brothers and a sister. This family-order business is no doubt part of our dynamic, the weird meshing of our two personalities. While Big Kenny's dad raised cattle, John's father, Jim, was (and is) a nondenominational preacher by calling. This was a tough living in those parts, so to make ends meet John's dad worked as everything from a night watchman to a car salesman during

ABOVE TOP: John and his sister Jamie.

ABOVE: John and his siblings: Jamie, Joy, and Isaac.

the week. John grew up in a trailer on the outskirts of Amarillo, and life got pretty rough sometimes. His family made more than one stop down at the local food bank. Again, two different people, two different life experiences.

John's dad, originally from Pampa, Texas, had aspirations early on in his life to do exactly what John does now. He loved to sing and write songs and play the guitar and would make a habit of performing church songs at weekly services from behind his pulpit. John would often sit beside his dad while he belted out a hymn or gospel tune, and by the age of five or six he was playing alongside. This was the catalyst for John's lifetime in music—watching his dad perform for and inspire the congregation on a Sunday morning.

To this day, John admires his dad for going his own way and never asking the world for permission. He's the kind of unabashed country preacher who rides his Harley to church, attends to his flock, then comes home, sets his King James Bible down on the table, and, as a final gesture, pulls up his pant leg and takes his .32 special out of its ankle

**ABOVE TOP:
John and his dad,
Jim Rich.**

**ABOVE: John at
his thirtieth
birthday party
with his dad.**

strap and puts it away. He's an original.

Today John's dad preaches in Tennessee and lives only a short distance from John. Also nearby are his beloved Granny Rich and Pap Rich, his father's parents. Granny Rich isn't just John's granny. She's *everybody's* granny.

After his upbringing in Amarillo, John ended up in the Nashville area by default. He moved to Ashland City, thirty miles northeast of Nashville, with his mother, a native Tennessean. He had a chance to go to college on a vocal scholarship but opted instead to try his luck in the "business."

EVERYONE'S GRANNY

She's in her seventies, and women who are eighty or ninety still call her "Granny" Rich. She's Big Kenny's adopted granny, Gretchen Wilson's adopted granny, Cowboy Troy's adopted granny—in fact, the granny-in-residence to the whole Muzik Mafia. She fixes them home cooking when they need it and comes to their concerts to cheer them on. She also makes and alters John's stage clothes, all those crazy rhinestone britches and the like. Granny's husband of fifty-seven years, "Pap" Rich—now eighty and fighting colon cancer—is a highly decorated World War II veteran. He owns six Purple Hearts for his service as a "tunnel rat" fighting the Japanese in underground bunkers. If you want to know where John gets his fierce love of country, drop by and say hello to Pap Rich.

ABOVE TOP:
John and Granny Rich.

ABOVE & LEFT:
Granny Rich adorns John's stage clothes.

THE LOVE OF MUSIC

What brought us together, of course, was music. We both felt the same way about music. We both grew up listening to every kind of music there was. Big Kenny came to playing music much later in life than John, but he loved singing in church, learned the guitar by listening to blue-grass, and had two older brothers who exposed him to a whole spectrum of popular music. Growing up, music was just something he loved and absorbed, never guessing that it would become his life's work.

John was known growing up in Amarillo as "Johnny Jukebox." He took to the guitar at the tender age of five, memorized the chords and lyrics of every song he could, and then played them right back at the next family get-together. To this day, he can sing all seven verses of Johnny Horton's classic "Sink the Bismarck." One of his childhood heroes was John Anderson of "Seminole Wind" fame, a man he's now producing! As a teenager, he could sing every John Anderson song ever recorded. Like Big Kenny, John was drawn to bluegrass. When he was eight, he'd go down to the local Wal-Mart to buy the cheapest cassettes he could find. The bargain ones were always bluegrass.

Our musical tastes growing up were not dictated by a single genre. Given the breakout of adventuresome, format-busting FM radio in the late '60s and '70s, a whole world of styles and formats were available to us with a flip of the dial. FM, of course, was just the forerunner of the vast musical universe any kid has access to today on iPods and the Internet. Back then, there was nothing called rap or world music or electro-pop or Latin pop or a dozen other forms now common to anyone with a computer, satellite radio, or MP3 player. But there was plenty for both of us to listen to as teenagers—from Stevie Wonder to the Electric Light Orchestra—much of it rooted in the American grain of country and blues.

Big Kenny was (and still is) especially fond of '70s rock and roll, listing some of his favorite groups at the time as the Steve Miller Band and Queen. But if he was a rocker, he was a rocker of a different breed. Blue-grass, traditional country, R&B, blues, even disco—it's all in his musical brain somewhere, and given the freedom of expression that is the hallmark of Big & Rich, most of those influences come out one way or another.

Inspired by whatever we heard, we both discovered early on that we had abilities outside traditional country music. To this day, if we are so moved, we'll try to write a great AC/DC or a great Tony Bennett song as much as we'll try to write a great Ralph Stanley and His Clinch Mountain Boys song. Or maybe something that is a blend of all three. As Big Kenny likes to say, "There are only two kinds of music—good music and bad music." We shoot for the former, no matter the style or genre. The philosophy is simple: Music without boundaries. All genres accepted.

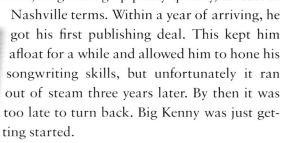

"There are only two kinds of music— good music and bad music."

✳

STUMBLING AROUND

No one in Culpeper believed Big Kenny when he said he was going to Nashville for good. They thought he'd be back in a month or two and get back to doing "real" work. Though he didn't have a clue how to make it in the music business, he got a leg up pretty quickly, at least in

Nashville terms. Within a year of arriving, he got his first publishing deal. This kept him afloat for a while and allowed him to hone his songwriting skills, but unfortunately it ran out of steam three years later. By then it was too late to turn back. Big Kenny was just getting started.

Big Kenny took on no other gainful employment in Nashville besides writing and playing music, so paying the bills became a bit of a problem. By this point, he had his own band— Big Kenny—and they were working the clubs as best they could. With little income, Big Kenny did what any red-blooded American would do in this situation—he put it on his credit card. Back in Culpeper, making an honest living in construction, Big Kenny had established some pretty decent credit. So now he took a huge risk and "invested" it in his music career. Music meant everything to him then. And, except for his love of family and friends, it still does.

When Big Kenny finally got his first record deal in 1998—a solo deal with Hollywood Records, Disney's rock label—he had more than one hundred thousand dollars in credit card debt. The solo album that was the fruit of that deal—*Live a Little,* recorded in 1999—shows off Big Kenny's true rock-and-roll

side. It also includes a solo rendition of the second song Big Kenny and John ever wrote together, **"I Pray for You."** Before Big & Rich the performing act, there were Big & Rich songs, and this is one of the most memorable to both of us.

OPPOSITE PAGE: Big Kenny at Lake Tahoe, California.

ABOVE: Big Kenny and Atomic Adam in their LuvjOi days.

Still, as records and recording deals go, Big Kenny was soon broke again. *Live a Little* just sat on a shelf at the record company gathering dust. As Big Kenny likes to say, he recorded his first album in 1999 and first heard it on a CD player in 2004. Until we hooked up and signed the first Big & Rich deal in 2004, Big Kenny just kept keeping on. He went from the Big Kenny band to the same band with a new, catchier name, LuvjOi—what normal people would spell *lovejoy*. In fact, John, though not part of the group, came up with the name. John and Big Kenny were playing at a buddy's wedding when Big Kenny asked him what he should call his new group. "Lovejoy," John said, "because that's what you're all about." So one night it was Big Kenny, and the next it was LuvjOi.

Big Kenny is great at the art of reinvention. LuvjOi was just a reconstituted Big Kenny, but the new name gave him a whole new way of looking at things. If you keep reinventing yourself, you keep rolling instead of losing faith and ending up lying on the couch in the middle of the day.

LuvjOi became the core of what would later become Big & Rich's first-rate band. Adam Shoenfeld, affectionately known as Adam the Atomic Guitarist, now the B&R lead guitarist, played with LuvjOi, as did drummer Larry Babb. We did leave behind one occasional element of the LuvjOi experience—an all-purpose variety act called Sideshow Benny. Benny would come out and wow the crowd with such stunts as drawing a dartboard on his back and having an assistant throw darts into his flesh. If that didn't getting 'em going, he'd pull out a box of five-inch carpentry nails and drive a handful up his nose.

Big Kenny tried to find other work from time to time, but nothing worked out. At one point he tried to get a job as a bartender, but was turned down because he didn't have any experience. He claims that he would have been one of the best bartenders in the history of mankind because of his almost limitless love of mankind. On the other hand, he would have probably given half the drinks away for free.

So the credit card bills started to mount up again. It wouldn't be until the first payday from the first Big & Rich deal that Big Kenny would start paying back a whopping $140,000 in debt. He was willing to bet the ranch, so to speak, on the success of Big & Rich, and I guess we wouldn't be writing this book if that bet hadn't paid off, big time. But we're getting ahead of ourselves.

LONESTAR DAYS

John's first bid to make it in Nashville opened the way for the next six or seven years of his life. At the bright age of eighteen—ironically, about the same time that Big Kenny first pulled into town—John auditioned for a show at Opryland called *Country Music USA*. It was a live, outdoor concert show where young talent gets a chance to impersonate legendary country singers. He initially thought working at Opryland might be a good summer job before college. After he passed the audition and got the job, he thought this was it—he was on his way to stardom.

Many current country stars, it turns out, got their start at Opry-

John and his Granny Rich.

land—members of Diamond Rio, Little Texas, and Restless Heart, to name a few. While performing in *Country Music USA*, John ran into a fellow performer named Dean Sams. Dean kept talking about a band he was trying to put together and wondered if John, with his ability to sing high melody and play the bass, would want to be part of it. The group got together to rehearse a couple of weeks later—and the band Lonestar was born.

Actually, the band was first called Texassee, a tongue-twisting combination of *Texas* and *Tennessee*. The group hit the road in a broken-down two-door Jeep Cherokee pulling a U-haul trailer to play country dives everywhere; they kept it up for two and a half years before their first record deal. John was a good ten years younger than the next youngest member. Because he was only nineteen or twenty, many bars wouldn't allow him to get off the stage between sets.

John had never been in a band before Lonestar, and in fact had never played with a drummer or stage monitors. It was all brand new to him, and he soaked it up. Lonestar served as his musical finishing school.

With the first check John received from his Lonestar work for "Come Cryin' to Me," which reached #1 in 1996—in fact the first big check he'd ever received for anything—he went out and bought a house in the countryside outside Nashville. Since he was on the road two hundred or more days a year, he asked Granny and Pap Rich if they would live there and take care of the place. They were going through a tough period at the time, so they were happy to make the move. They live there to this day.

After six years with Lonestar, John and the group had a major falling-out. John was all of twenty-three years old and wanted to play rock and roll and kick out the jams. The four older members had a more traditional country bent. One argument led to another, and in early 1998 John got his walking papers.

Do things happen for a reason? Is there some universal force moving people around and heading them in the right direction? If Big Kenny hadn't gone belly-up in the construction business and John hadn't been booted out of Lonestar, we probably would have never met, let alone partnered up. We had to fail, in other words, before we could succeed.

By the end of his six-year stint with Lonestar, John was a fairly well-known singer-songwriter in Nashville. Still, he wasn't sure exactly what direction his career would now take. Big Kenny knew who John was—he had seen him perform with Lonestar in a showcase down at the Wild Horse Saloon in the early 1990s. But John had no idea who Big Kenny was. Not until his girlfriend at the time dragged him down to a place called Douglas Corner one fateful night.

John situated himself in the back of the room and listened to Big Kenny sing and play. His initial reaction: "Well, it's some creative stuff, no doubt, but this guy doesn't have a chance in hell at doing anything in

Nashville. It's so out there . . ." The girls in the audience were screaming and having a good time, John remembers, but that's no recipe for success in tradition-bound Music City.

"Well, it's some creative stuff, no doubt, but this guy doesn't have a chance in hell at doing anything in Nashville. It's so out there . . ."

✳

At the end of the set, Big Kenny, feeling "everyone should leave the show with a little something," took his standard bag of bubble gum and slung it into the crowd. One of these fastballs hit John square in the face. John was perplexed at the whole situation.

Nevertheless, a mutual friend, Cindy Simmons, insisted we meet backstage. As John puts it, **"We looked at each other, kind of like two bird dogs the first time they met each other, sniffing each other trying to decide if they're going to fight or play."** At Cindy's further insistence that we get together and try to write something, we exchanged numbers and said good night.

After three canceled appointments, we finally got together to see if there was any creative chemistry there. We worked out a pretty good song that day and decided to try again the next. That next day was October 10, 1998, and we sat down and wrote **"I Pray for You."**

That was the beginning of the songwriting team Big Kenny and John Rich—and a lasting friendship—but a long way from the duo Big & Rich. For one thing, we both were at that point working on solo record deals with two different labels: Big Kenny had his rock deal with Hollywood Records, and John had negotiated a solo country deal with BNA Records. John, having left Lonestar, was now hell-bent on doing it alone. Big Kenny had pretty much always done it alone. Early on, the idea of performing as a duo never crossed either of our minds.

But the writing definitely clicked and led the way to what was to come. We knew we were different—much different—but we also learned that our differences and collective grab bag of musical influences seemed to make the songwriting more challenging and more productive.

THE MATCHMAKER

Around the same time that Big Kenny met John, and vice versa, Big Kenny met a man who would be central to the creation of Big & Rich as well as one of our best friends for life, TV and event producer Marc Oswald. As Big Kenny tells the story, he woke up one morning in 1998 in Marc's pool house at his lakeside home outside Nashville. The night before, Big Kenny, his friend Kurt Taser (better known as Pappy), and a couple of young ladies—nurses by profession—had come to Marc's house to party, though Marc wasn't at home at the time. This was all fine. Marc had given Pappy a key to the place just for such occasions. John had known Pappy from their Lonestar days, and introduced him to Big Kenny, a connection that would eventually change Big Kenny's and John Rich's lives.

The young ladies had driven home, leaving Big Kenny and Pappy

stranded. No problem. They each hopped on one of Marc's Jet Skis and skied across the lake to the house of Marc's brother—William Morris Agency agent Greg Oswald. There they borrowed Greg's Jaguar convertible to get back to town. Later Big Kenny returned to Marc's to thank him for the hospitality and brought along his guitar in case music was called for. It inevitably was, and a lifelong friendship was born.

If you ask Marc about his first impressions of Big Kenny, he'll say he found him fun loving, full of laughter, and "larger than life." Big Kenny, Marc says, had an expression in those days that gave you a damn good idea about where he was coming from.

> ### *"The ground is my floor, the sky is my ceiling, and the world is my one big happy home!"*

✳

"The ground is my floor," Big Kenny would announce, "the sky is my ceiling, and the world is my one big happy home!"

Eventually the conversation between Big Kenny and Marc that day turned to business. Big Kenny told him he wrote and sang songs, like the ones he had just been singing. Marc then asked him what, if anything, he had going. Big Kenny's answer: a deal with Hollywood Records. And the rest, as we'll soon see, was history.

And it all began with a wild night with two nurses.

OPPOSITE PAGE: It was through Pappy that Big Kenny and John Rich met Marc Oswald, the man who would be key to the formation of Big & Rich. Here he is showing off his catch while fishing with Big Kenny and Gary Chapman.

ABOVE: Marc Oswald and Big Kenny.

MARC OSWALD

BELOW: John, Marc, and Big Kenny visit the Mayan ruins in Mexico.

Born in Palo Alto, California, and a certified paramedic before moving to Nashville, Marc has been involved in various aspects of the music since 1981. He currently manages (with Dale Morris) us, Gretchen Wilson, Cowboy Troy, Randy Owen from Alabama, John Anderson, and Mista D. If Big Kenny hadn't crashed at Marc's lake house that night in 1998, there might never have been a Big & Rich. Then again, Marc was almost obsessive in making us see that we were a duo-in-the-making. Marc is always pushing the envelope, from videos to documentaries to our faces on ten zillion Pepsi cans. If there is a third member of Big & Rich—similar to manager Brian Epstein, the famous fifth Beatle—it's Marc.

WHEN PLANETS COLLIDE

Marc Oswald likes to say we are "the yin and the yang." We're not quite sure what he means by that, and which is yin and which is yang, but we are well aware, and grateful, that we are not clones of each other.

Just look at us on stage today. Big Kenny is often out there in a wife-beater T-shirt and a Panama hat, or a top hat, or no hat at all. John is his cowboy compadre, almost always wearing a fine cowboy hat, usu-

ally black, and the tailored jacket, shirt, boots, and rhinestone Wranglers (courtesy of Granny Rich) to match. He also has a fondness for bling. Big Kenny will tell you that he is always open to change. John will tell you that he is a hard man to get to change his course.

"Big Kenny likes to smell the flowers; John likes to mow them down."

Big Kenny has, in John's term, good "peripheral," meaning he picks up on things out of the corner of his eye, or ear, and quickly integrates them into his life. John is more directional. As he once told Gretchen Wilson, the first and only Godmother of the Muzik Mafia, "I am a pit bull who won't stop until you get your shot in Nashville." What does that make Big Kenny? Maybe some kind of a freewheeling canine, a globe-trotter, like a golden retriever. To quote Bob Dylan, "If dogs run free, why can't we?"

Cowboy Troy, a longtime member of the Big & Rich entourage, remembers someone once describing the difference between Big Kenny and John this way: "Big Kenny likes to smell the flowers; John likes to mow them down." John doesn't exactly see himself as a flower killer. In his own words, he would describe himself like this:

The pirate gypsy.

"I'm a real tunnel-vision kind of guy. Nowadays I'm trying to maintain my tunnel vision and increase my peripheral vision at the same time."

There are other differences between us, too. Big Kenny likes the open road, that's for sure; Marc Oswald calls him a "pirate gypsy."

"He's a gypsy," says Marc, "because he loves music and is just as happy on the tour bus traveling down the road or at a campsite at twelve thousand feet in the Colorado Rockies, cooking beans over an open flame, as he is watching TV in the den.

"And he's a pirate," Marc goes on, "because he lives by a pirate code." Take to the ocean, lift your mug high, sing a drunken chantey, live a lusty life, and steal from the rich and give to the poor. Or at least buy everyone in the world a mug of beer.

John likes to see the world as well, and he can hell-raise and outparty

Two goofy guys.

anyone in earshot of a bottle of Crown Royal. But right now in his life, he doesn't have much time for vacationing. In fact, when he's not working, he's probably working on something else. He's producing someone else's new CD—Jon Nicholson, John Anderson, Cowboy Troy, or Gretchen Wilson— or developing Rich Texan Music Publishing, which has a roster of six writers. He's plowing a new field.

But then you can flip things around and find John off partying and Big Kenny working non-stop on something like Damien Horne's (aka Mista D) solo urban rock, street pop album, or a collection of bawdy pirate songs for his son. Two planets always in orbit and often different orbits. It's a weird dynamic at times, but it works.

As we continued to write and hang out together, we realized that we had some pretty serious things in common as well. First of all, we are both anomalies in the country music business. We're both a little too rock and roll, a little too convention bending or, in many cases, flat-out convention ignoring. Not only are we ourselves anomalies, we are both "anomaly chasers." We search out people who are eccentric, iconoclastic, or just plain weird and try to draw them into our little sphere. Where other people see a freak or an outcast, we see a diamond in the rough.

One quick example. One of the members of the current Muzik Mafia, Mista D (aka Damien Horne), came to us, or we came to him, at two o'clock one morning when John was wandering around the streets of Nashville looking for his car. Mista D, a recent transplant from North Carolina and now an ordained minister, was parked on a street corner,

MISTA D

Born Damien Horne in Hickory, North Carolina, Mista D, a member of the Muzik Mafia since 2002, is a boundary-breaking urban singer-songwriter. *Mista D* is an acronym for "Musically Inspiring Souls to Always Dream." His singing career began in a Salvation Army church at age twelve. Fate, or maybe the hand of God, took him from North Carolina to the streets of Nashville, to Tuesday nights with the Mafia, to his current recording and touring career. He also just completed a degree in Christian ministries from the Free Will Baptist Bible College in Nashville and had the distinct honor of marrying Big Kenny and his lovely wife, Christiev, high on a hill outside Deadwood, South Dakota.

all alone, with a guitar and dreadlocks down to his beltline. He was just sitting there singing Bob Marley songs to himself.

John Rich is a big Gretchen Wilson fan.

John listened for a minute, knew this guy had something serious going for him, and impulsively invited him down to a Muzik Mafia get-together the following Tuesday. Mista D came, sat in with the rest of the rowdy crew, and soon became a permanent fixture of the Mafia. Big Kenny is now producing his first record, a blend of urban rock and street pop.

Mista D, along with many other talented people described in the pages to come, is an excellent example of the kind of anomaly chasing that we both specialize in. Neither of us hesitates to invest his life in people that we believe in, regardless of musical category or what anybody else says about them.

We're guys who bet on the long shots, the hundred-to-one shots. That's what we do. We don't bet even money. We bet on the horse that barely makes it to the race.

So we have our differences—a lot of them—but our common love of music, and people who play their own music, trumped those differences from the get-go. We knew something was working with our songwriting. The stage was set, but the recording and performing version of Big & Rich was still some way off. That came about, in time, through the weekly gathering of Nashville oddballs and misfits affectionately named the Muzik Mafia.

How to Write a Song

✳

Having been selected ASCAP Artist/Songwriter of the Year two years in a row, John knows a few things about writing successful songs. So does Big Kenny, who won the 2005 BMI Songwriter of the Year award. Both are happy to pass along a few nuggets of songwriting wisdom.

1. Your very first line has to be memorable. It has to make the listener anxious to hear the second line. It has to be unique and *new,* not a cliché. Clichés immediately dull a listener's response. Here's the opening line to Gretchen Wilson's "Here for the Party": "Well, I'm an eight-ball-shooting double-fisted-drinking son of a gun." Are you now sufficiently worked up to hear the next line? Here it is: "I wear my jeans a little tight / Just to watch the little boys come undone." And we're off!

2. Find the pocket. *Pocket* is a musician's term for the rhythm of a song and the rhythm of the lyrics, often as important as the lyrics themselves. The pocket is the groove—it's what gets your head bopping up and down. If you want to write a Big & Rich–style song, you'd better find a serious groove, whether it's a slow or fast song. The variety of pockets we bring to our music are often what make it different from other country music.

3. Pay attention. We get a lot of song ideas from observing life around us and feeling a connection to other people's stories. Like "Holy Water" or "8th of November." You don't have to be a Vietnam vet to understand what someone like Niles Harris has gone through—suffering and loss are universal. Or sometimes our songs come directly from our own sordid lives. "Save a Horse (Ride a Cowboy)" is a Big & Rich party handbook, and trust me, we've been to that party.

The lyrics to "Love Train" as recorded in Big Kenny's journal.

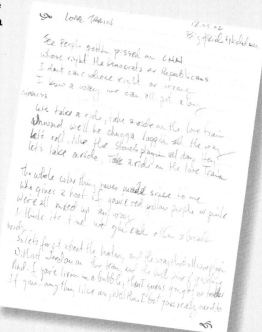

MUSICALLY ARTISTIC FRIENDS IN ALLIANCE

BIG KENNY: "What we realized when all of these people started coming out of the woodwork was how many people out there liked a little more diversity in their music."

JOHN: "We created an atmosphere of acceptability for oddballs. Sorta like the characters in the classic movie *The Dirty Dozen* or the famed maniacs of the 1970s Oakland Raiders."

The Muzik Mafia, the ragtag collection of unique and talented musician friends and collaborators probably most responsible for the birth and early feeding of Big & Rich, was conceived—where else?—in a bar. It was the creation of four friends now known affectionately as the original "Godfathers": the two of us plus R&B/rock/country singer-songwriter Jon Nicholson, and music publisher and executive Cory Gierman. We were all steeped in the same eclectic musical mix. Big Kenny and Jon Nicholson roomed together at the time, and we were all unemployed and discouraged by our many failed attempts to gain some creative traction in Music City. Nashville can be an awfully lonely place when you're trying to make

The Muzik Mafia.

Big Kenny with Jon Nicholson.

it on your own, and especially when you get kicked in the head, which was happening to all four of us simultaneously. As Cory remembers one of us saying at the time, "Man, is someone telling us to go home or what?"

We were all sitting around one night at a drinking hole called 12th and Porter, bemoaning the fact that music in Nashville was so segregated and pigeonholed. If you wanted to hear Big Kenny, for instance, you'd have to go to a rock club. If you wanted to hear John, you'd have to go to a country place. Since we were all friends and wanted to hear one another, then, we decided we'd get together periodically in one place and play together. If we were all going down, we figured, we'd go down together. We made an informal pact—no competition. Only cooperation and mutual support.

"We were all dreamers—Nashville is a gathering place of dreamers."

✳

As Cory likes to point out, we were all dreamers—Nashville is a gathering place of dreamers—and we needed a way of reigniting our dream of musical independence. We were tired of bumping up against a world of manufactured music. Out of our profound frustration in trying to get the Nashville deal makers to take any of us seriously, we fantasized about the prospect of using time-tested Mafia strong-arm tactics to get things done on Music Row. If only we could kick open a few doors, throw a demo CD on some executive's desk, and politely inform him that this was going to be his next big release. Maybe even bring him a nice baked ziti or ricotta-pineapple pie as a symbol of our friendship. Assuming the correct Tony Soprano–style attitude, no guns would have to be drawn and no kneecaps would have to be broken. We'd just move into the territory and run the show.

Or at least we'd get together, play some music, have a few laughs, and give one another all the support and encouragement we could muster. Out came the name *Muzik Mafia*.

Big Kenny's wife, Christiev, likes to tell the story about how the Muzik Mafia came to mean more than just "Mafia." The group had been up and running for a while and on the way to establishing itself as a Nashville underground phenomenon before Christiev entered the picture. The word *Mafia* was already a permanent part of its name and identity. But Christiev, of proud East Coast Italian descent, was bothered by this. *Mafia* was an Italian term that stood for something important to her, namely "Mothers and Fathers of Italian Americans," as she was taught as a child. (Other experts

The original Mafia napkin.

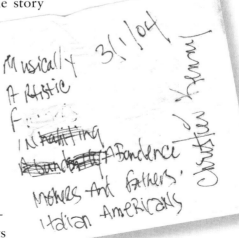

JON NICHOLSON

One of the original Godfathers, commonly known as "King," Jon was rooming with Big Kenny and working with Cory when the Mafia was born. Originally from Madison, Wisconsin, he grew up listening to Willie Nelson and Merle Haggard in one ear, and the Sex Pistols and Suicidal Tendencies in the other. His music is soulful, funky, country, all of the above—Sly Stone meets Leon Russell—and he has toured with everyone from 3 Doors Down to the Bob Marley Roots Rock Reggae troupe. His first album, *A Lil Sump'm Sump'm,* was released by Warner Bros. in late 2005, and he's currently at work on a combination live performance CD and DVD being produced by John Rich. All the usual Mafia suspects will show up to help out.

think it is an old Sicilian dialect word meaning "boldness" or "bravado.") In any case, Christiev thought, if that word was going to represent a group of Nashville musicians, it should stand for something.

Since Big Kenny had just started dating Christiev when this topic came up, he readily agreed to her astute analysis. So, on a cocktail napkin, they concocted the appropriate acronym of *m-a-f-i-a* for the Muzik Mafia: "Musically Artistic Friends in Alliance." This spelled it out nicely.

And given the additional connotation of boldness or bravado, it was the perfect word to describe something that started out as a fun way to spend a Tuesday night with friends and, over time, morphed into a permanent Nashville institution.

The Muzik Mafia: Musically Artistic Friends in Alliance.

✳

THE PUB OF LUV

After a few loose Mafia "sit-downs" at one another's homes, we decided that the group needed to go public. We needed a weekly gathering place to draw other like-minded souls into our conspiracy. The place we found was the Pub of Luv, a little bar across the street from 12th and Porter that had a tiny upstairs room no one was using on any given Tuesday night. The Muzik Mafia started using it every Tuesday night, from 10 PM to whenever, and kept gathering for the next seventy-six straight Tuesdays in a row. By the time we had decided to move to larger digs, the Mafia had become something we never imagined.

We chose Tuesday because, in terms of musical performances in Nashville, it's the deadest night of the week. This is the night that record executives and other players in the business stay home with the kids. On almost any other night, any number of industry showcases or songwriters' events are going on, the rooms usually filled with professional listeners with their arms crossed, trying to figure out if whoever's playing is good enough to get into business with. This makes for a pretty stilted musical environment. The people on stage are up there almost begging for a nibble, and often competing with the guy next to them for one of the very few slots in the recording business. The

The original Pub of Luv sign, which now hangs in Big Kenny's home.

deal makers in the audience are sitting on their hands, judging. A lot of the time, it's damn uncomfortable for all involved. If anything, music is supposed to be fun, and the typical industry outing in Nashville is far from fun.

So our idea was simple, and almost revolutionary, given how uptight the whole culture in town had become. We would just gather on Tuesday nights and see what the hell happened. It was not the dog-eat-dog environment of professional outings. It was more dog-playing-with-dog. In essence, it was nothing more than a bunch of friends getting together, like showing up in someone's rec room, and fooling around with music in the freest way possible. We'd mix styles and genres for the hell of it, going from a bluegrass riff to a reggae one. No one was making rules or keeping score. The only requirement was that you could write, sing, or play, but not get on stage and do a drunken off-key version of "Your Cheatin' Heart." It was a tribe of serious, and seriously open-minded, musicians.

As we constantly told one another, we were out to conquer the Nashville world with a completely different approach and attitude toward music. We were out "to beat the Man." Marc Oswald envisioned "the entire Muzik Mafia performing in front of ten million fist-pumping people in Tiananmen Square in Beijing, China, who probably can't understand a word. The good news is Cowboy Troy raps a little in Mandarin." We would stop at nothing less than world domination!

Our first official show was on a Tuesday night in October 2001. We took this nondescript room over the bar and tried to make it as warm and friendly as no money could buy. We went with the Salvation Army–living room look. We dragged a few couches and chairs up from downstairs, rounded up a few candles, threw a ratty rug or two on the floor, sat down, and started playing. "Showtime" was when the first chord was struck.

At first it was the three performing Godfathers—us and Jon Nicholson—playing with maybe a bongo drum or two behind us and a girl with a tambourine off in a corner. There was no stage, just a playing area. The "sound system," so to speak, consisted of some gray microphones, two rinky-dink speakers, and a starter-kit sound board that John would run while he played. Cory's job was to hang out in the audience and let us know if someone wandered in who might want to join us on stage for a song or two. It could be a street musician or a known star. We were always on the lookout for a mix of styles and performers we'd never seen.

The gaggle of onlookers were young—under thirty, mostly single, with nowhere they had to be on Tuesday night. The price was right: free. Many people, both on stage and off, had never been to an event remotely like this. This was not a Nashville showcase. This was a party. The smoke was thick, and the atmosphere was loose and unpredictable. If you didn't know someone, you just introduced yourself. For all you knew, you might end up writing a song together. It was a place where creative connections could be made.

For the next year and a half, the format on stage stayed pretty much the same. A group of musicians, usually including John, Big Kenny, or Jon Nicholson, would sit down in front of mics at the front of the room. Someone would start with a song they had just written. Someone else would pick up the same key, hopefully, and accompany them on another guitar. Then someone else would start singing harmony or backup. Then someone else would feel the spirit and start doing some free-form dance. This would go on for hours until everybody got too tired to play anymore. Then we'd dismantle the living room and go home.

And it grew. Pretty soon a second generation of Mafiosos joined the organization, namely rock/blues singer James Otto and a hard-shelled bartender-singer from the Bourbon Street Blues & Boogie Bar named Gretchen Wilson (she became the first Godmother). Everybody who wanted to participate was welcome, as long as they had the goods. You were either known by the principals or maybe left a demo for them to listen to. This was not an open-call tryout for *American Idol* or *Nashville Star*, though, ironically, it was in fact the breeding ground for a number of Nashville stars-to-be, including Cowboy Troy, co-host of what else? *Nashville Star!*

CORY GIERMAN

An original Godfather, the only nonperformer in the Mafia, leader of all Mafia Soldiers, settler of family disputes, and self-described glue of the organization. Raised in Becker, Michigan, and Fort Myers, Florida, Cory is now a partner in Raybaw Records and helps oversee the careers of Cowboy Troy, John Anderson, James Otto, Jon Nicolson, and all unsigned Muzik Mafia artists. Cory keeps the Mafia flame alive in a hundred different ways, from the Muzik Mafia concerts, to the award-winning Web site, to next Tuesday night's gathering of the tribe.

Somewhere along the way, both of us got new nicknames that we've carried with us since. Big Kenny became the Universal Minister of Love, a title he was born to wear, and John got tagged one Tuesday night as the Cowboy Stevie Wonder. At the time, John was up front playing an original barn-burning R&B composition called "Modern Disco" and channeling the Bee Gees through country through rock and back again. It prompted someone to say, "Man, you are grooving like Stevie Wonder in a cowboy hat!" It was the highest possible acclaim for a Panhandle Slim kind of a cowboy rocker like John, and he took it as a badge of honor.

MUZIK WITHOUT PREJUDICE

PHOTO BY MARK SE

HOME · ABOUT · NEWS · ARTISTS · MUZIK · ON TOUR · INTERACT · MMTV · SHOP · SOLDIERS

FEATURED

CMT LOADED

Catch MMTV on CMT!

Become A MafiaSoldier

Click here to sign up for our email list and be the first to receive news about behind-the-scenes video, Mafia shows and more!

GO

MuzikMafia

radio

Muzik Without Prejudice

GO

MuzikMafia *Auction*

Bid on exclusive ticke signed memorabilia, and more!

CLICK HERE!

ARTISTS   VIEW ALL

GRETCHEN WILSON

The Mafia Godmother almost didn't return John Rich's calls....

MORE

BIG & RICH

Getting big and rich hasn't made the duo any less freaky or fun....

MORE

COWBOY TROY

Welcome to the emergent era of music known as "hick-hop...."

MORE

LATEST NEWS   VIEW ALL

December 04, 2006
The Otto Show
Monday, December 11th. 12th & Porter. 7PM. Join James for a night of holiday cheer and southern ROCK. Details
MORE

November 30, 2006
MMTV Episode VII on CMT Loaded
This week Deanna Kay brings us a performance by Godfathers Nicholson and Rich and an in-studio visit from Rachel Kice. WATCH NOW
MORE

November 27, 2006
Gretchen's New Book For Sale
Just in time for Christmas, Gretchen's new book, "Redneck Woman: Stories From My Life," is on-sale in the

EMAIL UPDATES

Sign up to get all the lates news on Mafia artists!

GO

ALL ACCES TELEVISIO

MuzikMafi

THE WRECK

In the middle of the initial Muzik Mafia mania, Big Kenny had a life-changing experience—a brush with death. As he drove his truck home late one summer night after a session at the Pub of Luv, a drunk driver ran a red light and T-boned him, spinning the vehicle around in three or four complete revolutions. Big Kenny himself hadn't been drinking because he had spent all evening performing, and when he's doing one, he's usually not doing the other. Nonetheless, the wreck was a totally surreal experience—all the more so because he walked away from it with no cracked skull or broken bones. It was as if an angel had come along, wrapped around him, and kept him from harm. His first thought when the truck stopped spinning was, *Why am I still alive?*

The back and neck pain from that wreck, unfortunately, is permanent. Every time it flares up, it reminds Big Kenny of the moral of that late-night accident. Highly simplified, the lesson is that you can't prepare for the twists of fate that life might have in store for you; you can only deal with them and move on. If you do constant battle with your misfortunes, they will defeat you. Your task is to accept them and move on. Keep moving forward.

> ## "Come on down. You never know who's going to show up."

MAFIA SOLIDERS

Meanwhile, back at the Pub of Luv, the crowds got bigger, the music got louder and stranger, and soon our little jam-and-groove session took on the atmosphere of a carnival. With all the candles strewn around and people hanging off the stairwell and on window ledges, the place was a weekly fire marshal's nightmare. It became a badge of honor for people to say, in retrospect, that they were there for one of those notorious Pub of Luv shows. Cory stepped up as the linchpin of the organization, alerting fans to get-togethers, making people who came feel at home, and managing the changes unfolding in front of them.

The weekly on-stage show got stranger. Our slogan became, "Come on down. You never know who's going to show up." Which was true—we had no idea who might come through the door. A guy named Scott Neri the Juggler started appearing and marveling us with his sideshow antics, like scaling the wall outside and waving to people through the window. Major stars like Wynonna, Josey Scott from Saliva, or Martina McBride would come by to sing and play. Famous Nashville singer-songwriters—Jim Lauderdale, Mark Collie, and Kenny Beard, to name a few—made a habit of appearing. One night, an artist named Rachel Kice popped in and started doing chalk drawings on paper on the floor in front of the performers. As she finished one, Big Kenny would show it to the crowd. Over time, the chalk drawings became "live" oil paintings on an easel, and Rachel became the official Muzik Mafia visual-artist-in-residence.

Jon Nicholson and Gretchen Wilson perform while Rachel Kice paints.

Inevitably, the Tuesday-night crowd started to include first-tier record company executives who heard about this Tuesday-night musical tailgate party and jamboree, and decided to check it out for themselves. We weren't on stage to get a record deal, but playing like that, week after week, gave all of us a dose of confidence that we badly needed to keep going. And word got around.

Every Tuesday was unique. The cavalcade of guest performers was often downright weird. At a later show we did at a bar called Bluesboro, funk/soul/blues genius George Clinton—mastermind of Parliament-Funkadelic, or P-Funk—showed up to jam. Jon Nicholson had played a little with him on the road, and George returned the gesture. At the far other end of the music spectrum, one of the original "outlaw country" stars, Billy Joe Shaver, came by one Tuesday and ended up spending some time in the studio with us. The Muzik Mafia was (and is) an ongoing, ever-changing musical smorgasbord.

One night Cory was scanning the crowd and saw a long-haired dude with tattoos all over him checking things out. This was not a typical Muzik Mafia–looking guy. Someone nudged Cory and told him who he was: Josey Scott, lead singer of the hot, Memphis-based alternative metal/hard rock/post-grunge band Saliva. He had apparently heard the music while sitting across the street at a bar and followed the crowd in to see what was going on.

Before long, Josey was up on stage, playing together with people of a much different musical bent and having a great time. This was not something he had planned on doing on a night out in Nashville. At the end of his performance, he announced to the crowd that he was moved by the whole experience and that he was going away as a certified "Mafia Soldier."

GRETCHEN WILSON ON THE MUZIK MAFIA

"...It can get awfully lonely in Nashville when you're trying to make it on your own. Lonely and discouraging. During some very unstable and confusing times in our lives, the Muzik Mafia kept us all going. Because we were all in the same boat at the time, we were naturally inclined to support each other and help each other through the rough spots. I think it's fair to say that if each of us had had to make it on our own, only a few would have survived."

From Redneck Woman: Stories from My Life *by Gretchen Wilson (New York, Warner Books, 2006).*

John and Gretchen, the early days.

After that, a lot of people began to call themselves "soldiers." It was a burgeoning army of freaks.

What struck us as the most normal thing in the world—musicians gathering for the simple pleasure of playing music—soon became a kind of cultural watershed to which people started comparing everything, from the psychedelic "be-ins" of the 1960s to Willie, Waylon, and the outlaw country movement of the 1970s. Magazine covers such as *Country Weekly* and *Entertainment Weekly* were shouting: "The Muzik Mafia Wants You!" What we had done, apparently, was create a refreshing counter-environment to the uptight, commercially obsessed world of Nashville at the turn of the twenty-first century. People all over town were still making music, but few appeared to be having any fun doing it. If every time you get on stage for a showcase, your whole life and career depend on it, it's a little hard to just cut loose. The Mafia created a public place where cutting loose was not only allowed, it was damn near a requirement.

The "old" Muzik Mafia of the Pub of Luv days is long gone, but the group prides itself on remaining mutual friends, supporters, and collaborators. We still gather together on any Tuesday possible to just play music for music's sake. We did more than thirty-five Muzik Mafia Tuesday-night free-for-alls in 2006. The last one included John Anderson's induction as an honorary Muzik Mafia member, and an impromptu performance with Richie Sambora of Bon Jovi (Jon Bon Jovi also attended). Industry-wise, we didn't end up breaking any kneecaps or destroying any corporate offices Soprano-style, but we somehow managed to finally get in the door. And when that happened, all hell broke loose. The almost simultaneous mainstream success of Gretchen and yours truly put the Muzik Mafia on the big map.

AMERICAN REVOLUTION TOUR

Soon the group was no longer just a loose gathering of friends allied in music—it was a road show! People wanted to know about this strange-sounding collective out of which came these "overnight" successes. *USA Today* dropped by to write a big story about us. Then CMT called and announced they wanted to do *Muzik Mafia TV,* a six-part series that would follow the whole tribe around and film us together, apart, on stage, and just hanging out. The Mafia was now coming to your town.

The first official Muzik Mafia tour, called the American Revolution Tour, hit the road in November 2004, going to fourteen cities and playing before tens of thousands of new fans. A note of thanks to our friends at Chevy for helping us pull this off. It was a world apart from Tuesday nights at the pub. Jon Nicholson and James Otto would open, third-generation Mafioso Shannon Lawson would weigh in on part of the

JAMES OTTO

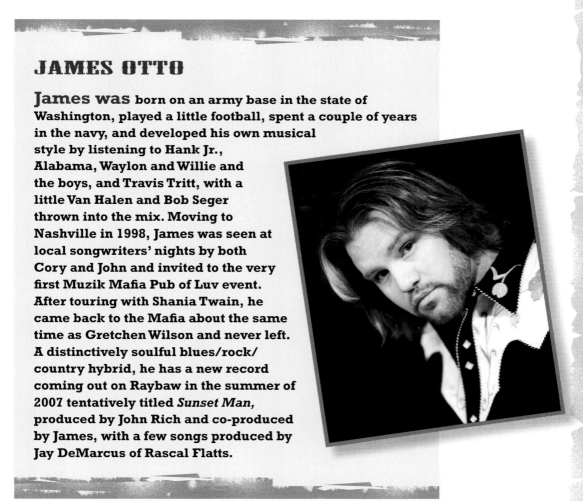

James was born on an army base in the state of Washington, played a little football, spent a couple of years in the navy, and developed his own musical style by listening to Hank Jr., Alabama, Waylon and Willie and the boys, and Travis Tritt, with a little Van Halen and Bob Seger thrown into the mix. Moving to Nashville in 1998, James was seen at local songwriters' nights by both Cory and John and invited to the very first Muzik Mafia Pub of Luv event. After touring with Shania Twain, he came back to the Mafia about the same time as Gretchen Wilson and never left. A distinctively soulful blues/rock/country hybrid, he has a new record coming out on Raybaw in the summer of 2007 tentatively titled *Sunset Man*, produced by John Rich and co-produced by James, with a few songs produced by Jay DeMarcus of Rascal Flatts.

ROCK & R

400

RIC

MBNA
Mid-Race Leader Award

Raybestos
OFFICIAL BRAKES OF

USG

GOODYEAR

WM
WASTE MANAGEMENT

Mobil 1
OFFICIAL MOTOR OIL & LUBRICANTS

NASCAR
NEXTEL
CUP SERIES

GOODYEAR #1

3M

Holley
HP CARBS

FOOTWORD

EA
SPORTS

MECHANIX WEAR

GOODYEAR EAGLE

OUTBACK
STEAKHOUSE

Gillette MACH3
Turbo

CLEVITE

JESEL

Auto
Meter
PERFORMANCE GAUGES

COMP
Edelbrock

30

Big & Rich enjoy NASCAR and were excited when the Chevy Cingular car was designed especially for them.

AN AMERICAN

COLOR

tour, and Gretchen and the two of us would headline. Cowboy Troy also performed, of course, as did Two Foot Fred and our artist-in-residence, Rachel Kice.

We were truly a traveling road show now—nine buses full of old friends and partners, five semi-trailers carrying a lot more than a couple of couches and some candles, and a full, twelve-man video production crew from CMT filming us every time we decided to get out and zip around on Harleys before a big show. We had a ball. On stage at the House of Blues in Las Vegas, James Otto proposed to his girlfriend, Amy Alderson. In the middle of our Texas leg, we stopped off to say hello to Willie Nelson. The CMT crew came back with seven hundred hours of Muzik Mafia footage.

In all, we were on the road for five weeks. For many people in the Mafia, this was the very first time they'd ever been part of such a huge musical caravan, going from Fresno, California, to Evansville, Indiana, playing arenas and dealing with thousands of adoring fans.

In a way, this first tour was the logical culmination of what the original four Godfathers fantasized in that first conversation at 12th and Porter. The dream was: Someone hits it big and everyone profits. Now we were literally living the dream as a group of mutually supporting artists. Soon Jon Nicholson was recording his first album, *A Lil Sump'm Sump'm*, with Warner Bros. Records and touring with everyone from Kid Rock to the Marley Brothers on their Roots Reggae Tour. Other artists like James Otto and Shannon Lawson were headed toward new deals. And Cory Gierman was looking for new heights to conquer.

ABOVE: John Rich's Muzik Mafia Godfather ring, not for sale.

OPPOSITE: John representing the Muzik Mafia.

RAYBAW RECORDS

American Revolution Tour I led to American Revolution Tour II and various other collective bookings. Besides the touring and the TV mini series, there soon emerged the whole Muzik Mafia organization—the

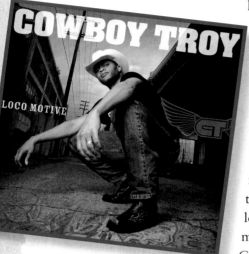

Web site, recently honored as one of the best music sites on the Internet; the publishing company; and all the merchandising, from T-shirts and license plate holders to Muzik Mafia rings. According to Jon Nicholson, the only way to get one of those rings is to bump off one of the nonperforming soldiers wearing one. Or maybe find one for sale on eBay.

Today the active core of the Muzik Mafia fans—otherwise known as Mafia Soldiers—numbers more than fifty thousand. They travel all over the country to meet up with fellow soldiers at Mafia events. They are in constant communication with one another through forums and chat rooms on MuzikMafia.com. Together they help us perpetuate the Mafia's mission to spread the love of music and to help others while doing so. Mafia members have been involved in everything from the Crohn's & Colitis Foundation of America, to the Muzik Mafia Country Music Hall of Fame benefit at Ryman Auditorium in Nashville, to raising money for Hurricane Katrina relief. We're out there and we're getting bigger every day.

Cowboy Troy's first album, *Loco Motive*, debuted at number two on the country charts, selling fifty thousand units in the first week.

The four original Godfathers decided to take the process a step farther and create a record label that would continue the Tuesday-night tradition of giving exceptionally promising, and so-called unconventional, new talent a place to record.

"All genres accepted."

What we created, with the help of Warner Bros., was Raybaw Records. *Raybaw* stands for "Red and Yellow, Black and White." This is not just an announcement of our desire to invite anyone of any ethnic persuasion into the show. That's a given. It also means that we want to run a label that refuses to bar any style of music of any kind from consideration. When we say "All genres accepted," we're not just spouting a slogan. We're trying to build an all-inclusive record company.

To us, a more diverse musical output in Nashville is a natural evolution from the original "Music City." Nashville is increasingly multicultural. Asians and Hispanics are moving to a town already 25 percent African American. There are professional sports teams here now, and a brand new state-of-the-art symphony center. It's only natural that the image of Nashville's music change along with the image of Nashville. It's both inevitable and healthy.

Paul Worley at Warner Bros., our biggest supporter in the music business, helped us create this imprint with a unique mandate. We find and record an act—any act—and the many branches of Warner Bros. will find a place to market and promote it. Pop, urban, country, gospel—we are free to move in any of those directions. Country is of course our bread and butter, so as we develop a new country act, we go to Warner Nashville. But if we find a techno act we love, we go to Warner London; an urban act, Warner Los Angeles. It's a unique arrangement in the music business and continues the tradition we began sitting around the Pub of Luv on Tuesday night: Everybody's welcome, as long as you've got the goods.

The first artist to record on Raybaw was Cowboy Troy, a perfect choice for a new record label dedicated to diversity. Troy's country rap (aka "hick-hop") CD, *Loco Motive*, came out in 2005 and has sold close to four hundred thousand copies without any significant amount of radio play.

John is currently producing Mafia member James Otto's first album for Raybaw. In addition, one of country music's legendary singer-songwriters, not to mention one of John's idols— John Anderson—will release his next album on Raybaw. We'd love to take on more artists, but we don't have the re-

John Rich with former president of Warner Bros. Records Jim Ed Norman, and Paul Worley, head of creative affairs at Warner Bros. Records in Nashville.

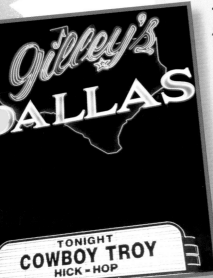

TONIGHT
COWBOY TROY
HICK - HOP

PUT YOUR BODY IN MOTION!

"Dum-diggity-dum, diggity-diggity-dum, dig this
Slicker than the grease from a barbecue brisket
Got more chunk than a fresh potato salad
You thought you had your answer but your answer
*   wasn't valid*
You're lookin' at me crazy 'cause you think I'm loco
The Big Black Cowboy with the crazy vocal
Todas las personas están gritando arriba
Now you heard it, now I know you're a believer
Esta canción es para toda la gente
Es muy importante a usar su mente
So let go of all your preconceived notions
Get up on your feet and put your body
*   in motion . . ."*

Lyric excerpt from Cowboy Troy's rap in "Rollin' (The Ballad of Big & Rich)."

sources to do so. Our main interest is seeing that our friends get recorded, not necessarily get recorded on Raybaw. However it happens, it all comes back around to help us all.

The interconnection of Mafia members has moved from the stage to the recording studio. Kentucky-born, third-generation Mafioso Shannon Lawson is a perfect example. He brings a rocking bluegrass element to the group—hence his nickname, Atomic Bluegrass. As a performer, he's a part of the Muzik Mafia traveling road show. As a songwriter, he works with the two of us via Muzik Mafia Publishing, our publishing arm. He has one original song on the new Gretchen Wilson record and four songs on the new John Anderson record; he sings with James Otto on his new record. As you can see, Shannon is very involved.

HOW THE MAFIA ROLLS

The Muzik Mafia takes this customized limo to special events. Each door bears the name of one of the four founding godfathers: **Godfather Big**, **Godfather Rich**, **Godfather Nicholson**, and **Godfather Gierman**.

Shanna Crooks, another member of the Muzik Mafia, joined in 2005 when she signed a publishing deal with John Rich. A singer-songwriter from South Florida, one of her nicknames is Bling Queen. John is quick to call her "one of the best songwriters I've run into in a long time." Her music is a soaring blend of pop/rock/soul, and her lyrics range from soulful to the kind you can't help but sing along to.

THE POINT

One of the great things that has happened in the wake of the Muzik Mafia is the emergence of other groups of like-minded Nashville musicians who have joined together to create their own musical universe, such as the Movement, Dirt Pharm, and Trailer Choir. It's contagious. The Muzik Mafia happened so fast that a lot of people were caught off guard, if not inspired, by its meteoric ascent.

"Wait a minute! Weren't those the knuckleheads who were playing at the Pub of Luv last week?"

The Muzik Mafia celebrated its fifth birthday on October 21, 2006. That's a bit astounding to us. It was, after all, just a frolic among friends, a way of getting together to enjoy one another's music and company. The fact that it lives on is a wonder to us all and more or less a vindication of our original goal—to help one another. Success, in other words, was a way to shine the light on our friends and not just take the money, glory, and private plane, then stop returning their phone calls. If anyone in the Mafia had succeeded and not stayed connected to and supportive of the others, then the whole tagline of "Musically Artistic Friends in Alliance" would have been pretty much BS.

But that hasn't happened. No one has gotten too big for the Mafia. We still get together, pitch songs back and forth, draw new and often untested talent into the group, and look forward to the day when another soldier breaks through and we can all celebrate another collective victory.

World domination! Long live the Muzik Mafia!

Do You Know the Muzik Mafia?

*

Do you know which Muzik Mafia artist is which?

<table>
<tr><td>1. Big Kenny</td><td>A. The King of Hick-Hop</td></tr>
<tr><td>2. John Rich</td><td>B. G-Dubb</td></tr>
<tr><td>3. Cory Gierman</td><td>C. Atomic Bluegrass</td></tr>
<tr><td>4. Jon Nicholson</td><td>D. Cowboy Stevie Wonder</td></tr>
<tr><td>5. Gretchen Wilson</td><td>E. Bling Queen</td></tr>
<tr><td>6. Cowboy Troy</td><td>F. Minister of Love</td></tr>
<tr><td>7. James Otto</td><td>G. The Otto Show</td></tr>
<tr><td>8. Damien Horne</td><td>H. The Deuce</td></tr>
<tr><td>9. Rachel Kice</td><td>I. Godfather G</td></tr>
<tr><td>10. Shannon Lawson</td><td>J. King</td></tr>
<tr><td>11. Two Foot Fred</td><td>K. Artist-in-Residence</td></tr>
<tr><td>12. Shanna Crooks</td><td>L. Mista D</td></tr>
</table>

ABOVE LEFT: "Full Frontal," a portrait of the Muzik Mafia painted in performance by Rachel Kice in 2004, acrylic on canvas 5' x 7', image © Rachel Kice 2006, collection of Michael Bowsher.

ABOVE RIGHT: Rachel Kice creates.

ANSWERS: 1. F, 2. D, 3. I, 4. J, 5. B, 6. A, 7. G, 8. L, 9. K, 10. C, 11. H, 12. E

HORSE OF A DIFFERENT COLOR: MAKING OUR FIRST RECORD

BIG KENNY: "We sat down in front of Paul Worley (at Warner Bros. Records) and about the third song we got to was 'Holy Water' and that was the one when he stood up at his desk and slammed his hand down and said, 'I want to do this! ...'"

JOHN: "And we said, 'Ah, want to do what?' He said, 'Want you to be the first act I sign on Warners.' And we went, 'Ah, listen ... could you repeat that, please?'"

THE BIRTH OF BIG & RICH

The Muzik Mafia provided a home for Big & Rich, or at least for Big Kenny and John Rich, two guys hell-bent on doing their own distinct thing. We were good friends by then; we'd write songs together and help each other out any way we could. We took one trip to LA where Big Kenny the rock star was about to get signed, stayed at the fanciest hotel on the Sunset Strip, and blew what little money we had on liquor and laughs. Out of this little adventure came the song **"Drinking**

The first annual meeting of the Big & Rich board of directors: Dale Morris, John Rich, Greg Oswald, Marc Oswald, and Big Kenny.

'Bout You." Big Kenny remembers on another occasion yelling to record executive Sam Ramage into a cell phone while we were traveling somewhere, "You are an absolute dumb ass if you don't sign John Rich!" It must've worked—the man signed John two weeks later, though it didn't exactly lead to instant stardom.

And of course we'd sing together on Tuesday nights, although two minutes later one or the other of us would be singing with Jon Nicholson or Gretchen Wilson or another musician du jour, or all of us at once. Both of us now with firm solo deals—Big Kenny a rock deal and John a country deal—the timing was not right to seriously consider pairing up. Of course, neither of us was ready to see ourselves as *faltering* solo acts—solo acts going nowhere fast.

ABOVE: John reenacts his reaction to losing his solo record deal on the very same truck he drives to this day.

OPPOSITE: The two Kennys: Chesney and Big.

We both needed someone to help guide our careers. Big Kenny had the help of Marc Oswald at this point. Marc wasn't a rock manager per se, but was still trying to get Big Kenny hooked up with someone from the rock world who would steer him to stardom. At this critical juncture, John had no manager, no savvy insider in his corner who could open a few doors for him. The perfect guy, John thought, would be Dale Morris, the big-time manager of stars like Kenny Chesney and Alabama, and a man both of us knew socially through Marc Oswald. We played a lot of music together around Marc's pool with Dale and many others listening in.

So Marc asked Dale if he would be interested in managing John, as Marc himself tells it. Dale said no, he had his hands full with Kenny Chesney and didn't want to take on another solo male country artist. But, as Dale told Marc after hearing us sing together one day, if Marc could get the two of us to team up as a duo, Dale would be willing to

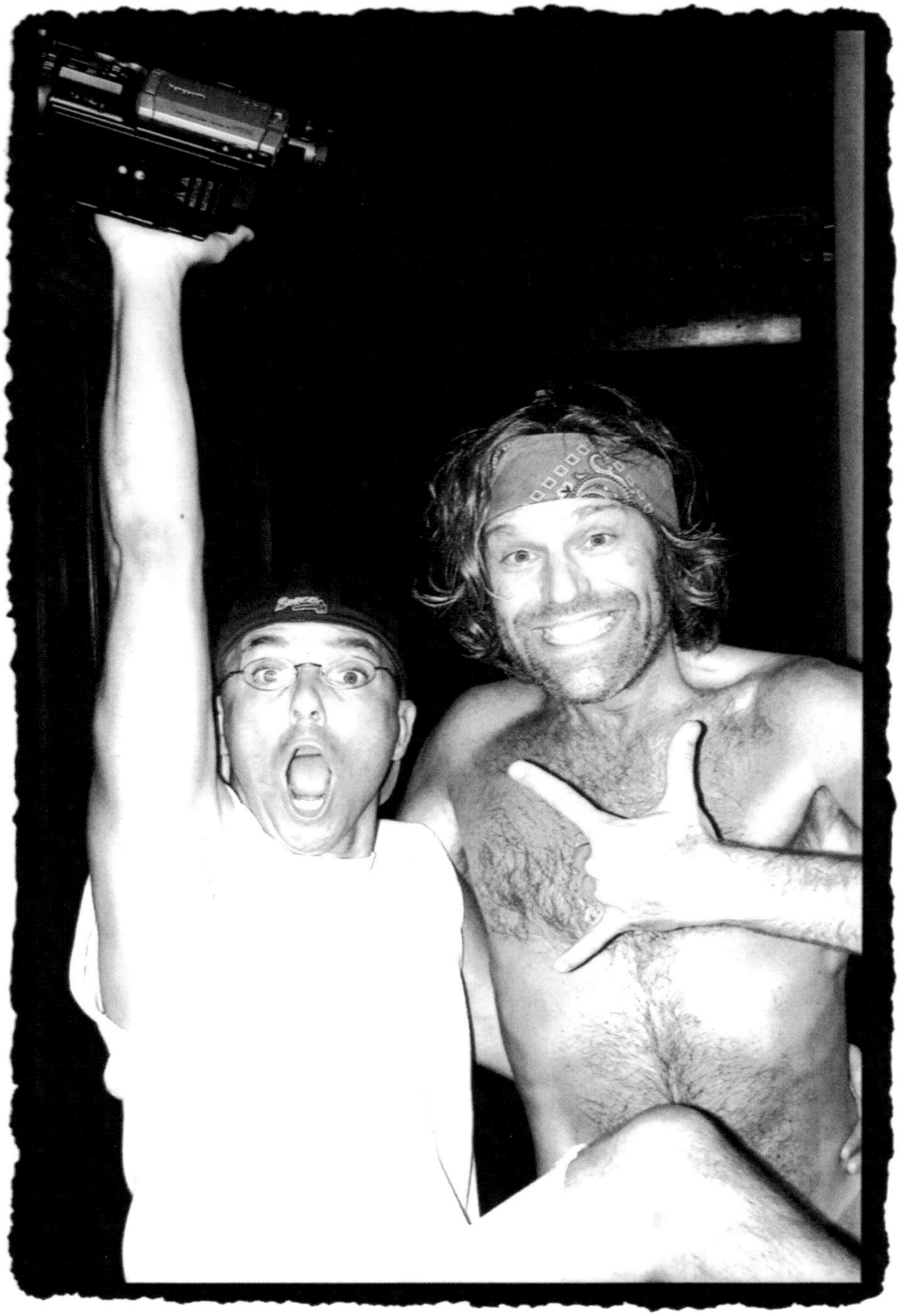

help guide our career. Marc heard Dale loud and clear, but hesitated to pitch the idea to either of us. He probably guessed that the answer from both of us would be a polite, "Hell, no."

Months later, Marc heard us sing together as Big Kenny and John Rich at a songwriters' showcase at the Bluebird Café in Nashville, a venue where a lot of country songwriters get a chance to show their wares to all the song buyers in town. The crowd reaction, Marc remembers, was over the top, not to mention that Marc himself was blown away. He figured now was the time to hit us with the duo idea. Now was the time to show his hand.

So he drags us out to his lakefront house the next day, fixes us omelets, and plies us with champagne. After an hour or two of that, he lays it on us: You guys should become a duo. You should become "Big & Rich," a country music duo.

"You should become 'Big & Rich,' a country music duo."

We both looked at him like he was a Klingon. John spoke first, and Marc remembers his exact words: **"You have got to be kidding me! My deal is over at BNA and they told me I'm too rock for country."**

"Right," said Marc.

Then John pointed to Big Kenny and said, **"If I'm too rock for country, what are they going to think of *that*?"**

That morning, Big Kenny looked pretty much like he always does: His hair was a bit unkempt, and he was wearing some kind of weird bandanna—in short, he looked about as far from a Music Row country artist poster boy as you could get. In fact, he looked a lot more like Tommy Lee than Randy Travis.

Big Kenny quickly said that he was going to make his rock thing happen and had no interest in being in a duo, let alone a country duo. From both of us, the answer was a quick and definitive "Hell, no."

So, cut ahead another eight or nine months. We were still good buds, still writing songs together, but still seeing ourselves as two distinctively different artists pursuing two different paths. Then Marc had an idea. He wanted us to work with some first-time songwriters on the art of composition and was willing to pay us to do so. Both of us needed the money and jumped at the opportunity. The MasterCard Priceless Edge program—set up by Marc—was an opportunity for college students from across the United States, ages eighteen through twenty-five, to be selected to come to Nashville for a monthlong music business and creativity seminar. We did it for two summers in a row, and it was a lot of fun. It brought us closer together as a team.

As part of that process, we decided to go into the studio and demo a few of songs we had written, both inside and outside the Priceless Edge program. We had written maybe a hundred songs together by that point and performed many of them on stage at writers' showcases, but never recorded together. That, it turned out, made all the difference in the world.

"If I'm too rock for country, what are they going to think of *that*?"

**"Holy Water"
video.**

Marc had no doubt about what he was hearing—a duo. And he knew everyone, even us lugheads at the center of this thing, would get it, too. When you are on stage performing live as a duo, you hear yourself and a bit of the other person. When you record together and play it back, you hear the two of you flat-out. Once you stand back about two feet, it's as plain as the nose on your face.

HOLY WATER

Big Kenny gave Marc the CD from those demo sessions; Marc stuck it in his bedroom player and out came **"Holy Water,"** a song we had written about, of all things, abuse. There were other key songs in our career on that demo, too, but "Holy Water" was the one that struck the deepest chord. Looking back, it was probably the song that ignited the whole crazy phenomenon.

Which is kind of fitting, given our desire to write songs that matter. "Holy Water" is not a typical country ditty about a broken heart, or dancing with your main squeeze, or memories of Mama back home. It's about men beating up their wives or girlfriends. And it's about the women who have been abused seeking comfort and redemption by being immersed in holy water and having it touch every part of their body and cleansing them.

It came directly from experience. Both of us have sisters who have been physically abused by men. One day we started comparing notes about this sad state of affairs and realized that a majority of the women we have known in our lives had faced abuse like this—not just our sisters, but women we've dated and even one of the co-writers of the song, the wonderfully talented Vicky McGehee. We wanted to shine a light on this all-too-common horror—but also point the way to a better place.

There's a spirit out there, the song says, that will surround you and pick you up and pull you out of this terrible situation. It will free you from guilt and shame. It will hold you "like holy water."

Some songs, country or otherwise, are much bigger than the actual notes and words. Think of John Lennon's "Imagine" or Bob Marley's "Get Up, Stand Up." "Holy Water" is one of those songs. The evidence of this is in the response it has gotten from the moment we started including it in our live show. Women constantly come up to us after a concert shaking and crying, often with long letters to us explaining how that one song gave them the courage to get out of a bad relationship or kept them from doing something drastic, like killing themselves. Of course, we didn't know that at the time we wrote it. We just knew we had written a song that meant something to us.

John and song co-writer Vicky McGehee.

Marc heard "Holy Water" and fell over. He then played the song to Dale Morris, and before it was through Dale again agreed to co-manage the duo. Marc called John first and said, "Dale wants to manage you." Before John could say "Wow," Marc added: "As Big & Rich."

John said, without hesitation, **"I'm in."** By this point the obvious was obvious, even to him.

Then Marc called Big Kenny, told him the same thing, and got the exact same response: **"I'm in."** Over that long period from the first time Marc had mentioned the duo idea, the two of us, writing and singing and even recording together, had actually *become* a duo. It happened so naturally we didn't even realize what was going on.

But the moment someone brought it up again, we both knew that, together, we might really get it going. And the catalyst was "Holy Water."

HORSE OF A DIFFERENT COLOR

As luck would have it—and by this point, luck was definitely along for the ride—we found the right label and record deal in a very short time, at least by Nashville standards. It wasn't the result of a big, orchestrated campaign to get signed. It wasn't a hundred public showcases or in-office auditions or polite turndowns. God knows we had paid those dues, individually and together as songwriters and performers, a thousand times over. It's as if we had both spent all those frustrating years in Nashville preparing to come together as this self-defined entity, Big & Rich.

The record signing was a fluke, really, a fluke of good fortune. Ashley Worley, the daughter of the man who had just been appointed head of creative affairs at Warner Bros. Records in Nashville, Paul Worley, liked our music and set up a meeting with Paul. The whole idea was to go in purely as songwriters and pitch him a few songs that might interest other artists on the Warner Nashville roster. No managers or agents were there, just the two of us. It was much more informal than most of your in-office pitch meetings. Paul politely listened to a couple of our songs and said something along the lines of "Great. I hear 'em. Let's go."

Our reaction was "Sure, ah . . . let's go where?" Paul then announced he wanted to sign us up as Big & Rich. In fact, we would be his first of-

The Deadwood
Welcome Wagon.

ficial signing in his new capacity at Warner Nashville. Paul had barely gotten there. He still had unpacked boxes sitting in his office. But he was ready to roll, ready to put Big & Rich on the map.

And that, to our astonishment, was that.

Paul Worley remains to this day probably our biggest supporter in all of the music business. Having played in rock-and-roll bands in college, he understood the musical mix we were attempting. And in terms of making things happen for us, he was, and is, formidable. He's like the biggest, baddest offensive tackle on the football team. He opens the big holes in the line that we can run through, assuming we don't fumble the ball.

Given the haphazard way things often happen in a high-pressure world like the music business, it could have easily taken us years to bump into someone like Paul who heard our music for what it was and didn't try to twist and turn us into a conventional country act that would go down easy with every radio programmer in America. Paul heard what Marc Oswald and Dale Morris, our then brand-new managers, had heard. The same thing probably a lot of other people heard before the two of us finally got it through our thick skulls: Big & Rich were ready for the Big Show.

DEADWOOD

Now all we had to do was come up with a dozen or so songs that we could put on our first album. Since we had first met in 1998, we had written literally hundreds of songs together. They were just songs that came to us, in any form. We never said, "Oh, this isn't a song that might get cut by, say, Garth Brooks, so we shouldn't be writing it." They were all manner of songs, ones that lyrically announce, *I'm not afraid to live this life through my dreaming eyes* or *Will I be the one you follow through eternity?* one minute, and *Why does everybody want to kick my ass?* the next. After signing with Warner, we simply redoubled our efforts to generate the best songs we could come up with.

"It's the storytelling in country songs that make them great."

We call these songs "country music without prejudice" for a reason, as opposed to, say, "rock and roll without prejudice" or "pop music without prejudice." It's the storytelling in country songs that make them great, storytelling about everyday people and their concerns, whether it's shopping at Wal-Mart or confronting God. People actually *listen* to country songs, in the same way they listen to folk music or a Bob Dylan song. Many rock and pop songs become big hits and fans have no idea what the lyrics are— they just like the rhythm and melody. They can dance to it.

We apply a lot of other musical forms and feelings to our songs, and

Big Kenny's journal entry of the lyrics to "Kick My Ass."

we certainly hope you dance to them, but when it comes right down to it these songs depend very heavily on their lyrical content to have an impact. **"Holy Water"** means little unless you know what it's about. We're not talking "Louie, Louie" here. If you don't hear and feel the words, the song won't hit its mark.

There is no other place in the world that has a bigger pool of extremely skillful professional songwriter-storytellers than Nashville, Tennessee. In terms of popular music, Nashville is the closest thing we've got to a modern Tin Pan Alley. Being surrounded by great craftsmen and -women forces you to raise the bar on your own songs. Otherwise you'll just get blown away by the competition.

Between our first record deal and recording the first album, we got a performance gig in Deadwood, South Dakota. Like a lot of things in our professional lives, it was something that was jumpstarted by Marc Oswald, who had visited Deadwood on a completely other matter. Deadwood now looms large in our hearts—among other things, this is where we met Niles Harris, the Vietnam vet and inspiration for **"8th of November,"** an unforgettable experience we'll get to later. At the time, we figured Deadwood would be like a retreat where we could forget about Nashville for a few weeks and just write what came to us. It turned out to be one of the smartest things we've ever done.

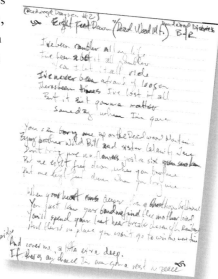

The lyrics for "Deadwood Mountain" as recorded in Big Kenny's Deadwood Diaries.

Even before we took off for Deadwood, we came up with the first single we ever put out there: **"Wild West Show."** We were sitting around John's apartment one day, getting all excited about our adventure to backwoods South Dakota. We both loved the whole idea of the mythical Wild West—gunslingers, buffalo, tepees, and peace pipes. So we became absorbed with all that rich imagery and ended up using it to write a song about a completely different subject: an argument between a man and a woman.

The chorus is this battle of the sexes in Western terms:

*"It was a big showdown,
oh, yeah we stood our ground
Shot out the lights,
It got a little crazy . . ."*

To us, it was the perfect way to describe the fireworks of a knock-down-drag-out argument between people who love each other intensely. Which led us to an obvious conclusion: If they were going to survive this struggle and stay together, they'd have to "smoke the peace pipe" and "forget about who's right or wrong."

What started as just an appealing list of cowboy-and-Indian images from growing up in America quickly turned into something that might apply not only to warring couples, but also to warring friends, warring in-laws, and even warring nations. The same general principle applies in all cases.

Simply stated,

*"Only forgiveness will finally end this,
There won't be a witness if we both fall
There's never a hero in a battle of egos,
There's never a winner in the quick draw . . ."*

Without those lyrics, and the meaning behind them, "Wild West Show" is just a nostalgic ditty about the Lone Ranger and Tonto. With those lyrics, it became a *country* song, a story about learning to get along with each other.

One song we wrote while staying in Deadwood probably typifies the way we tend to take something from our immediate life, like most professional songwriters, and turn it into music. The song is **"Six Foot Town."** When you first listen to it, it might strike you as a giant metaphor about being hemmed in by small-town life. As the chorus goes,

"It's hard to get around in a six foot town
When you're ten feet tall, everything is so small."

This conjures up the image of an adventurous, creative person caught in Small Town, America, itching to get out and make a name for him- or herself in the Big City—a classic America scenario.

Here's what the song is really about, at least in its imagery. While in Deadwood, Big Kenny was given the beautifully ornate top hat he wears with pride; it was a gift from our friend Niles Harris. Like a kid with a brand-new Yankees cap, Big Kenny rarely took that hat off for the whole stay. The problem was, every time he walked through a doorway, the hat would come flying off and shake him up a little. He began to anticipate every threshold and duck way down before he got there. With that hat he was damn near ten feet tall in a six-foot town.

Even without the hat, when Big Kenny went to bed in the apartment over the bar where we stayed, his six-foot-plus body hung over the bed frame. One night of this discomfort and by the next morning, he had the makings of a song. Shortly thereafter, we were partying with some Indian friends and decided to help them clean up the mangy apartment. A broken TV sat in the corner, and before you knew it, Big Kenny and John were tossing it out a two-story window into the middle of Main Street, just to see what kind of crash it would make. Or—to quote the song—

"When I step to the window and I toss a TV
Sometimes I get crazy and it makes a big scene."

An old Zenith, we came to discover, "makes a big boom."

So we mixed all that stuff together and out came a song about a guy with way too much zest for life to hang out in this place where people live in tiny boxes and worry about mismatched socks. Good songs, as we continue to tell aspiring songwriters, come from real life. "Six Foot Town" is a perfect example of that.

One more Deadwood tale. We had barely started to identify ourselves as Big & Rich when we made that trip. It was like the early stages of a marriage, after the initial euphoria—"Is this thing really going to work or not?" Well, one night while we were hanging out in our brothel slash hotel room, Kenny stepped out of the shower, walked into the next room with a towel around him, and announced to John, "Come see this." He pointed to a steamed-over window and said, "Hey, don't you see it? It's an image of Jesus!"

John saw no such image, but didn't want to burst Kenny's bubble. Kenny went on: "Not only is there this image of Jesus, but Jesus also spoke to me."

"Really," John said. "What did He tell you?"

"He said that everything in the world was going to get in between the two of us to make this thing *not* happen, and by God, we can't let *that* happen."

John immediately got the message. He never saw the image in steam, but he knew Kenny was right. At that moment, Kenny had received a powerful spiritual message that kept us both wary of dissension and petty bickering in those formative days. It's kept us together ever since.

On the set with the film crew of the "Big Time" video in Deadwood, SD.

SAVE A HORSE

A whole gaggle of songs that we wrote and recorded on both our first and second albums—including our first smash hit, **"Save a Horse (Ride a Cowboy)"**—came from working with those kids in the Priceless Edge songwriting program. Part of the process for them was getting to sit in a room with writers like us and try to come up with song ideas right on the spot. The trade-off was obvious—the kids could see how songs get written, at least in the early inspirational stage, and we would hopefully write a song or two worth keeping.

We were just grabbing ideas out of the air. One morning, John strolled into the room where we met with the kids and started passing out hundred-dollar bills. He had seven of them and just handed them to seven wide-eyed kids. One girl began to stick the bill in her bra when John said, **"Ah, hey, wait a sec—I'm going to need that back."** He was just making a point: namely, if you're going to be a professional songwriter, you got to get paid or you're dead meat. **"Feel that hundred, give it a smell. It's what you're going to need to survive."**

The kids loved it, even if they had to give the money back. Around the same time, we started a class by asking the kids if anything crazy had happened to anyone since arriving in Nashville. One girl from Texas spoke up and said she had been at the Wild Horse Saloon the night before when she got hit on by a cowboy. His line: "Hey, darling, how'd you like to save a horse and ride a cowboy?" The girl's reaction: "Can you believe that he said that to me?"

We looked at each other and said, "Yeah, we can." We intuitively understood that lecherous cowboy and his whole lusty slant on things. Both of us, at one point or another, had been that cowboy. And off we went on a song of the same name.

So we had a title, a subject, and an attitude—a cocky cowboy Romeo on the make—and ended up beginning the song with John's big-spender gesture.

"Well, I walk into the room
Passing out hundred dollar bills
And it kills and it thrills like the horns on my Silverado grill . . ."

Many other lyrical details in that song were inspired directly by these kids. As we were spitballing ideas, one black girl from Detroit chimed in that we should put something in about being in a club "bling-blinging." We asked for a clarification and she explained: "See, you know, like I would come in and big boys, you know, they'd come up to me all bling-blinging and all that . . ." We got it and soon had a lyric that gave the song a little urban twist:

"Well, I don't give a dang about nothing
I'm singing and bling blinging
While the girls are drinking
Long necks down."

Only in America can you put *bling* and longneck beer bottles in the same verse. It's all part of the same great cultural stew.

A number of other Big & Rich songs came from rubbing elbows with those bright, enthusiastic kids who gave us a taste of the real world outside the Nashville songwriting machine. In fact, one of those songs was titled **"Real World,"** about a guy who dreams of hooking up with the cute girl on Channel 13 while knowing full well that his real world isn't so glamorous. Other songs from the same period include **"Never Mind Me," "Leap of Faith,"** and **"Comin' to Your City."** It was probably the best thing you could do with two young songwriters like us—put us under the magnifying glass of those kids so we could be inspired to come up with something good.

At the end of one Priceless Edge summer session, we had all the kids down to the Pub of Luv to celebrate with the Muzik Mafia. We had no plans to ply them with liquor, but since a lot of them were underage, the management of the pub got a little concerned. We were getting fed up with the management at that point and we knew the students wouldn't be drinking, so we snuck them in over the back fence. It was a riotous night and in fact our last one at the pub. Having those wonderful kids around was a fitting way to end one chapter of our musical life and begin the next.

BROTHERS AND SISTERS

We finally had the songs we wanted to put out there and went into the studio to record them. We decided that we would invite Cowboy Troy to join us, both as a nod to his unique, high-energy talent and as a nod to the whole idea of a wide-open musical diversity we wanted to carry over from Tuesday nights with the Mafia. Troy was to become a regular and integral part of our stage show. When he walks on stage and starts rapping and dancing, the place always explodes. It was only fitting that he soon began work on his first solo album, *Loco Motive,* the first release from Raybaw Records. We loved having Troy around, but we especially needed him for the song—some might call it an anthem—that opens the album, **"Rollin' (The Ballad of Big & Rich)."**

"Rollin' (The Ballad of Big & Rich)" states upfront and point-blank what Big & Rich are all about:

AIN'T GONNA SHUT MY MOUTH!

"Country boys don't rock 'n' roll
Yeah the record man told me so
You'll never get it on the radio

Why they tryin' to complicate
The simple music that we make
Oh, 'cause it moves my soul, I'm gonna keep
*   on rollin', rollin'*

Ain't gonna shut my mouth
Don't mind if I stand out in a crowd
Just want to live out loud
I know there's got to be
A few hundred million more like me
Just tryin' to keep it free."

Lyric excerpt from "Rollin' (The Ballad of Big & Rich)"

"Brothers and sisters
We are here for one reason
And one reason alone
To share our love of muzikaaaahhhh!"

In other words, we open the album with a statement of musical purpose and not a rousing guitar lick (that comes about thirty seconds later). This is not a common record opening for any piece of popular music, and certainly not for a country album, let alone a debut country album.

We're announcing a musical philosophy—"country music without prejudice." Why start with such a blatant credo?

First of all, Big Kenny just likes to spout rousing preacher-like calls-to-worship like "Brothers and sisters . . ." It's part of his secret desire to be a black televangelist. More importantly, this anthem had to do with the way we had been misperceived for years inside the Nashville music industry. Before we banded together, we both had gotten sick and tired of hearing the same lame blow-off line and then being politely shown the door.

"John, you made this record and we think it's pretty good. You've made some great music here, but . . . but, frankly—what the hell is it? We can't figure it out. This is not rock and roll, and it sure ain't country. How can we market something like this?"

Or, "Big Kenny, we love the kind of music you're making, but we don't know what the hell to do with it. It doesn't, you know, fit anywhere. We don't know what to label it, how to promote it, what to tell the radio boys, nothing. Thanks but no thanks."

We decided that if we were going to combine forces and create Big & Rich, we were going to tell people right off the bat who we were and what they were about to hear. We figured that if we came out of the gate with a clear-cut message, they'd never again ask us—"What is this stuff?"

So we gave them a handle, a slogan, something to tell the marketing people and the promotion people and the radio people and, hell, their spouses. It's "country music without prejudice." Country music that consciously and willfully breaks the traditional bounds of what you might expect. Love it or hate it, but that's what it is.

And it must have worked. We've never read a review that said, "Big & Rich are a cross between this artist and that artist," or "Big & Rich sound like so-and-so with a little bit of so-and-so thrown in." Critics, apparently, and listeners, too, have simply dealt with the music on its own terms. The response is not always positive, that's for damn sure. Many country music purists think our music is warmed-over dog leavings or, at best, just a noisy mix of a whole radio spectrum full of influences. More power to 'em. Hey, you can't please everybody.

In hindsight, identifying ourselves from the very beginning was the smartest thing we could have done. The act of creating a winning image in Nashville is a critical part of the packaging and marketing of an artist. Something as simple as the right come-hither CD cover photo or the right pair of faded, hole-filled blue jeans can send a powerful message to a potential fan. Much of that image making is done by people at the record label, and too often the image ends up being a messy collage of a lot of different people's ideas of "what's hot" or just a phony representation of who the artist really is. Sometimes country artists have to spend years undoing a particular image before they can really come into their own creatively.

Since we didn't fit any already popular image to begin with, we sure didn't want a record label to force us into one. We didn't want to become this week's carbon copy of Brooks & Dunn. There was already a Brooks & Dunn, and they were great. So we told them right up front what the music was and why we looked and acted like we did. We didn't have to manufacture an image. We brought a real one—ourselves—to the party.

And when the country audience saw us as well as heard us, the whole issue just disappeared. "Oh, them? They're Big & Rich. They're a couple of wild men."

The King of Hick-Hop

✳

Cowboy Troy, aka Troy Coleman, first bumped into John Rich in 1993 in a club called Borrowed Money in Dallas, Texas. John was on the road with Lonestar and Troy was the only six-foot, five-inch black cowboy in the joint. As John remembers, Troy stepped onto the dance floor in Wrangler jeans and a "mo better" shirt, and began two-stepping with a hot-looking lady. By the end of the set, Troy had sashayed around that floor with at least ten hot-looking ladies. This was someone John had to meet.

Troy had grown up in Dallas, Forth Worth, and Austin, and took an early liking to country music. He listened to Jerry Reed and Charlie Daniels and hummed the Waylon Jennings opening to the original Dukes of Hazzard. That is, when he wasn't listening to and dissecting the styles of Run DMC and LL Cool J. Other people might have found this strange, but it made perfect sense to Troy.

Cowboy Troy's hick-hop belt buckle.

After getting a BA in psychology from the University of Texas and almost finishing a MA in economics, he fooled around in the nine-to-five world until he wandered away to write music. He sold shoes to stay alive and developed his own brand of country music at night—hick-hop.

John, being the anomaly chaser that he is, kept in touch with Troy and finally got him up to Nashville to meet Big Kenny and the rest of the Mafia. He played with LuvjOi and fit right

in with the eclectic Mafia crowd. Cowboy Troy—a black rapping Texas cowboy—had found a musical home.

Then it happened—boom, boom. From appearing on our first album and joining us on the road, out came his solo album Loco Motive, now with sales of more than four hundred thousand. Around the same time, he was asked to co-host Nashville Star, the breakout country talent show on the USA Network. Troy is the Muzik Mafia's first certified TV star.

Is Cowboy Troy, the modern-day Charley Pride, an anomaly or a trend? Maybe the trend in Nashville is a string of anomalies, and Troy is just out front leading the Hick-Hop Federation. Yee-haw!

LIGHTS, CAMERA, ACTION: ADVENTURES IN VIDEOLAND

BIG KENNY: "I think that the way that our music exploded and the way our first record exploded was word of mouth. There's no doubt in my mind that it was friends telling friends."

JOHN: "Our music is scary to some people in country radio ... we think, someday, radio will finally see what we're up to and that we're not the Antichrist of country music."

etween completing the first album and its release, we did what came naturally to us—we hit the road. Along with Marc, a documentary crew, and a still photographer, we loaded up and headed out West. We figured we could do all of the pre-release promotional stuff that new artists need to do and at the same time take in some mind-blowing American vistas. We could write our musical biographies, take still pictures, and shoot film of us singing and/or horsing around for what are known in the business as EPKs. *EPK* stands for "electronic press kit." This is video material that can be used in a hundred different ways, from sending it to radio people

On the set of the "Big Time" video.

ABOVE: We rented a couple of Lincoln Continentals, adorned them with old cow skulls, and took off down Baja.

RIGHT: At the granite falls outside of Yellowstone National Park.

as an introduction, to giving it to TV talk shows or entertainment news shows. We thought that hitting the road was the best way to show us as we really are, and simultaneously have a good time.

We were used to taking trips together. Whenever there was downtime, it was—and still is—our principal way to uncork. To this day, we go on short treks before shows, between shows, and after shows. Another trip we went on around the same time as the Western journey took us to San Diego, where a friend of Marc's by the name of Barbone was succumbing to cancer and wanted to throw a big wake while he was still alive to enjoy it. Before the party, we decided to take a little side trip to Mexico. We rented a couple of Lincoln Continentals, adorned them with old cow skulls, and took off down Baja. Big Kenny had a beard at the time that made him look like an Old Testament prophet or maybe a Mormon polygamist, or both.

On the Wild West photo shoot, we rode Harleys, climbed mountains, and played music, just the two of us and our guitars, wherever we felt like it. We rode horses across the Great Plains and up to some beautiful granite falls outside Yellowstone National Park, Wyoming, and sang to the great outdoors. We visited Jackson Hole, Wyoming, Livingston, Montana, and of course dropped in on Niles Harris and the rest of our newfound rowdy friends in Deadwood, South Dakota.

Deadwood was quickly becoming our home away from home. We'd be back plenty more times, to shoot music videos, do a documentary about Niles, dedicate a Vietnam War memorial, or simply to kick back at the local hangout, Big Al's Buffalo Saloon and Bodega Bar. When it comes to generating publicity material, some artists will spend weeks inside a professional photographer's studio or on some exotic, art-

We sat in front of Wild Bill Hickok's grave site and sang "Deadwood Mountain," dedicated to "my brother Wild Bill and sister Calamity Jane."

director-picked location to create exactly the image they want. We just took a road trip and brought back the true and unvarnished image of who we really are.

The photos and video from that trip were a telling introduction to Big & Rich. The West runs through all of our music. Our album was called *Horse of a Different Color*. The first single was **"Wild West Show."** The breakthrough hit was entitled **"Save a Horse (Ride a Cowboy)."** It all has to do with the imagery of the great American frontier. Seeing us roaming around that frontier was as natural and authentic as anything we could come up with. And a hell of a lot of fun!

FELLINI COMES TO NASHVILLE

Video is critical to what we do. Without our videos out there to help define, express, and bolster the music, we'd probably still be playing the Pub of Luv on Tuesday nights. If we had come up in the era before video was an everyday occurrence, we probably couldn't have taken the chances in country music that we have and succeeded. It could just be that you've got to see us to believe us.

The first single off *Horse of a Different Color*, **"Wild West Show,"** was well received but didn't prove to be the breakthrough hit we imagined. It made it up to the midtwenties on country music radio and then eased its way back down the chart. This didn't really surprise or disappoint us. Often in country music, it's the second or third single off the album that becomes the spark to ignite album sales. Programming singles for radio release is not a science. Like producing and releasing movies and TV shows, and almost any other creative work, it's a lot about hunches, and timing, and sometimes downright luck.

"Wild West Show," nevertheless, got us out there. Even as a top-twenty hit, it had a sound and style that reached millions of radio listeners through the stations that played it, which were a majority of country outlets. So, later, when we popped up on ESPN's *World Series of Poker* or some other unconventional media outlet, they could make the connection. Or if they bought a ticket to see Tim McGraw—there we were.

SADDLE UP!

Leading the Freak Parade.

BIG & RICH ON "SAVE A HORSE (RIDE A COWBOY)"

JOHN: "A lot of energy. A lot of T&A. A pivotal moment in everybody's career."

BIG KENNY: "Fun time, man. We made a parade. How many people can say they made their own parade?"

Shooting the "Save a Horse (Ride a Cowboy)" video in Nashville.

The next song we wanted to get out there, badly, was **"Save a Horse (Ride a Cowboy)."** Even before the release of the album, we knew we had to have a killer video to go with that song. Producers Robert Deaton, George Flanigan, and our own Marc Oswald stepped up to pull it off. Working with a veteran video director, David Hogan, and applying all the visual creativity in the room, we went for a big, big show of a video. Think of something by the legendary Italian director Federico Fellini, known for his wiggy, circus-like images, or maybe a huge movie musical like the Nicole Kidman hit *Moulin Rouge.* We were ready to pull out all the stops and shake up country music on all fronts.

The only problem was that our grand video fantasy cost a lot of money. The initial budget was four to five times the cost of a standard country video at that time. And the plan was to put it all up there on the screen. If you've seen the video, you'll know that it includes, among other things, a 120-piece college marching band; a troupe of dancing girls with half a dozen costume changes; Secret Service men; a team of cheerleaders; a convoy of Cadillac convertibles; two riding horses; Gretchen Wilson on a John Deere tractor; a two-foot dwarf; and a large black rapping cowboy. This is not a solo country star sitting on a fence post out at the farmhouse, singing a lonely tearjerker.

When we took the concept and budget to the record company, they laughed in our faces. When we came back with the same general concept but a budget half as big, they kept laughing.

Their attitude was clear. "With all due respect, boys, if you think we're going to spend that kind of money on an insane video starring a couple of brand-new artists who have yet to sell a *single record* . . . well, we'll get back to you . . ."

So we whittled the budget down as far as we could and set the dates to shoot the video, trusting that the company would see the wisdom of our ways. They didn't. Four days before the beginning of principal photography, they pulled the plug. They canceled the video. Everybody had to stop working. As far as the record company was concerned, this Fellini-esque pipe dream was dead on arrival.

We couldn't back out now. We couldn't let this perfect video for our (hopefully) breakout song just die on the vine. We got Carl Black Chevrolet, one of our major supporters from the beginning right through today, to help out. Then Marc and Dale Morris came to the rescue and funded the rest out of their own pockets. They agreed to pay half of the remaining production costs if the record company would pay the other half. This was a big risk on their part. If the song and/or album tanked, they'd never see their money again. We couldn't pony up the funds,

Dale Morris with his soon-to-be-superstars Gretchen Wilson, Big Kenny, and John Rich.

that's for sure. John was broke, and Big Kenny was still dealing with a $140,000 credit card balance. The fact that Marc and Dale had that much faith in us at that juncture—remember, we had yet to sell one album—still makes us feel good.

So we made the video. It was like a full-blown musical production, like something you'd see in the movie *Grease* or Fellini's *La Dolce Vita (The Sweet Life)*. The location we ended up using was the pedestrian bridge that runs over the river in downtown Nashville. We closed the bridge for twenty-four hours and shot the whole video in one eighteen-hour stretch. Because of the delay in shooting, we lost our original band—so at the last minute we lined up the world-class Pearl Cohn High School Marching Band from

ABOVE TOP:
Riding in the "Save a Horse (Ride a Cowboy)" video with the "living mannequin."

ABOVE:
Gretchen Wilson.

Nashville. We created a living mannequin—a young actress made up to look like an inanimate store dummy—to ride in a convertible and play footsie with Big Kenny. We got professional dancing girls from Atlanta and dressed some Mafia members up to look like Secret Service types. Add to that the horses and the tractor and Gretchen and Cowboy Troy. In the end, there were two hundred people marching and dancing around on that bridge that day. It felt like a cast of thousands.

Finally, we brought in a performer who would soon be a permanent part of the Big & Rich traveling circus—Fred Gill, or, as the world now knows him, Two Foot Fred.

TWO FOOT FRED, AMBASSADOR OF ATTRACTIONS

Fred and
Toby Gill.

Two Foot Fred—Fred Gill—hails from Seymour, Indiana, population eighteen-thousand-and-change. Fred is not a "midget," an old circus term that is more of a slur than a description. Fred and his brother, Toby—otherwise known as Toby Wan Kenobi—are diastrophic dwarfs and proud of it. Their parents are full-size. Go figure.

Two Foot Fred is really three feet, two inches tall. He is a graduate of Ball State University, and when he's not functioning in his official capacity as Big & Rich's Ambassador of Attractions, he runs, with Toby, the Funky Monkey restaurant and bar in Seymour; manages a couple of hundred rental properties they own; has a spice company (Fat Freddy's) and a text messaging service; and does a little acting on the side. John gave him the nickname Two Foot Fred so that everyone on the "Save a Horse (Ride a Cowboy)" shoot would instantly know who he was talking about. Now he's an integral part of the Big & Rich merry band of pranksters.

What does an Ambassador of Attractions actually do? Well, in addition to appearing in videos, Fred does a lot—he's a connection to the fans, to the media, and to damn near anyone who has a question about Big & Rich. He answers fan letters and greets people before and after concerts. He emcees our shows and usually brings the house down with his unique style of dancing during numbers like "Save a Horse (Ride a Cowboy)" and "Rollin' (The Ballad of Big & Rich)." When Fred gets down, it's an invitation for everyone in the audience to stop thinking about themselves and just cut loose.

John had first encountered Fred at Fan Fair, the huge annual Nashville festival, in 1999. Because of his long association with Lonestar, John was at Fan Fair, signing autographs at a booth, when this friendly dwarf ambled up to say hello. There was something about him that John liked, an X-factor of some sort. Fred was not just a man in an altered physical state. He was something else. In the same way that John had met Cowboy Troy in 1993 in a bar in Texas and filed him away in his memory box, he got Fred's phone number. He knew they would meet again.

When Fred walked on the set of the "Save a Horse" video some four years later, it was the first time Big Kenny had ever met him. But Big Kenny is a quick study. He could see right away that a fun-loving, hard-dancing, three-foot loony in a red cowboy hat and shirt, twirling a Mardi Gras parasol, was just what this video needed to put it over the top. And he was dead right.

THE TURNING POINT

"Save a Horse (Ride a Cowboy)" was definitely the turning point for Big & Rich, but not because it was an instant hit on the radio. Truth be told, the song never made it past number eleven on the national country music radio charts. It was heard, of course, and embraced by many a radio programmer, but it wasn't an automatic entry on a lot of country music playlists. When you think about it, it was a bit of a strange bird for a standard country format. It had a lyric line that sounded suspiciously like rap, and words like *bling blinging* next to *giggin' frogs* and *my old bird dog*. In retrospect, we are very appreciative that the song got the initial play that it did. Many people in the country music business were betting against it.

The video, on the other hand, took off like a rocket. It hit the top of the country video charts almost overnight and stayed there for weeks. It was the number one most requested video on CMT and GAC for four weeks in a row. We gave the audience the video we wanted, and it did the trick. The video was an apt expression of our whole musical outlook; rather than being just a backdrop to the song, the video *became* the

song, and vice versa. When you saw the video, you heard the song. When you heard the song, you saw the two of us, plus a couple hundred of our closest friends, having the time of our lives in the video. It just all melded together.

What we realized very quickly is that, in the age of iPods and the Internet and five hundred cable networks, our music was reaching people in a lot of different ways—via *The Tonight Show with Jay Leno*, as a catchy theme song for ESPN's *World Series of Poker*, broadcast on CMT.com, or by plain old word of mouth. We also had the distinct

Gretchen Wilson on the set of "Save a Horse (Ride a Cowboy)" video.

In the red-light district in Cologne, Germany.

honor, just as "Save a Horse (Ride a Cowboy)" and the album were breaking, to be asked to join Tim McGraw's Out Loud Tour. It's a long, long way from the Pub of Luv on a Tuesday night to a stadium of fifty thousand people singing along to every word of "Save a Horse (Ride a Cowboy)." However they did it, the audience for country music without prejudice found *us* rather than us being so clever and savvy as to find them.

Wherever we played that first year, it was the sheer passion of the fans that convinced us we were going to be fine. To this day, Big Kenny keeps a single postcard attached to his mirror at home to remind him what he gets up every morning to do. It's from a young girl, and the message is simple and direct: "Big Kenny, you are awesome. You inspire me in many ways. Never let anyone put you down. You are a great performer and human being."

When people telling people about your music is the principal way it gets out, the process can take awhile. It was a good eight or nine months

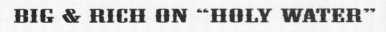

BIG & RICH ON "HOLY WATER"

BIG KENNY: "Compassion. Thinking about all the people out there who hopefully have people to pull them through."

JOHN: "The coolest thing was that Kenny's sister was in the video. I only wish my sister had been there, too. To have his sister fly out to LA and be in it made it all that more real."

from the time our first single was released to the time the album started showing high-volume weekly sales. On top of the "Save a Horse (Ride a Cowboy)" single and video, we also released singles and videos of **"Holy Water,"** the song that got us the record deal, and **"Big Time."**

Again, the same pattern emerged: The videos of those songs shot up to number one, while the radio play didn't reach the same level. Without video, in other words, it would've taken much longer to get our name out there.

The video of "Holy Water" couldn't be more different in tone and style from the "Save a Horse (Ride a Cowboy)" Freak Parade. The video begins with John standing next to an attractive woman and announcing: "This is Charlene, Big Kenny's sister, and we wrote this song for her and all the people out there like her."

The video has us singing the solemn, almost devotional anthem in a very straight-ahead fashion, surrounded only by water and the images of women who have gone through this awful experience. No marching bands, no bling-blingin', no live mannequins or dancing

The "Holy Water" video.

ABOVE TOP: Playing Trafalgar Square in London.

ABOVE: "Big Time" video.

dwarfs. It was important to us to let people know right away that our music often touches on things that touch us, and that "country music without prejudice" includes prejudice against women, too. At one point in the video, Big Kenny sings face-to-face with his sister. This underscores the point that this is a love song—not a romantic love song, but a family and friend love song. The video ends with Big Kenny holding up his guitar, showing his trademark message on the back: LOVE EVERYBODY.

On the "Big Time" video, we were back to goofing around, this time largely from the roof of the Franklin Hotel in downtown Deadwood. Intercut are images of other big-time moments, like playing in Trafalgar Square in London, snowmobiling in Crested Butte, Colorado, and hanging out on the back of a yacht in the Virgin Islands. One of the lyrics in the song fits these images to a T: " 'Cause I've got friends like you / To buy me drinks, and boats and planes that I can use." And this is true. Given the great and generous friends we have, we've got keys to summer houses and fishing boats from the Rockies to Nantucket to the Virgin Islands.

Big Kenny on the yacht *Lori Sue*.

ACROSS THE POND

As Kenny likes to remind us both, one of the reasons we got into music was to travel, both exposing the world to our music and experiencing the world firsthand. Not long after we started to break, we did some serious traveling. We took off to Europe on a promotion and photo tour, first to Germany and then to England. It was John's first trip across the pond, and it was all strange and wondrous. He remembers calling his Grandpa Pap from Cologne, Germany, to say hello. He said, **"Pap, I'm in Germany."**

Pap shouted back, "Well, get the hell out of there as fast as you can

and shoot everybody on the way out!" In Pap's mind, we were still fighting the Nazis and John was on the front line.

We thought we were a world away from Nashville and country music
until we were sitting in a bar one day in Cologne, drinking a glass of our
new-favorite German beer, Kölsch, and Keith Urban walked in. He was
staying in the same hotel, doing pretty much the same thing—spreading
country music across Europe. That encounter sure made the world seem
a lot smaller.

---

*"You're in the big time, no matter where
you are, as long as you want to be there.
A great thought on how to live life."*
—Big Kenny on the "Big Time" video

**Big Kenny and
John Rich hang
out with Keith
Urban in
Germany.**

We loved London. We made one of our first stops at the famous
Abbey Road Studios, where the Beatles recorded some of the greatest
pop music of all time. In the **"Big Time"** video, we threw in our own

mock version of the famous street-crossing photo on the cover of their *Abbey Road* album. If you look closely, you'll see that we even duplicated the VW parked in the background. John, in bare feet, stands in for Paul, Adam our guitarist plays George, and Troy plays Ringo. Also, please notice in the still version of this tribute image that Two Foot Fred is riding on Big Kenny's roller bag. Otherwise, he might have been run over by oncoming traffic.

Traveling to London and traipsing to that studio was definitely our version of "living in the big time." Like every one else who came by, we signed our names and Muzik Mafia to the wall in front of the studio. We moved all over London, from Trafalgar Square to Big Ben, and snuck

A tribute to the Beatles *Abbey Road* album.

Signing the wall
in front of the
studios where
Abbey Road was
recorded.

as many of those images
as we could into our videos.
In Trafalgar, we were surrounded by a big Christian
revival group rubbing elbows
with Goths, punks, and the
homeless. It was a real Big
& Rich environment.

How much fun did we
have in London? In five days
there, we ran up a bar tab
totaling a mind-blowing
twenty-five thousand dol-
lars. We bought drinks for
everyone we bumped into, all
the time. One night we ordered up thirty shots of super-
expensive King Louis XIII
cognac for our crowd. Hey, we
had just launched our very first
album and didn't know if we
would ever be back as Big &
Rich. As John said at one point,
we were going to "ride it out"—
and we did.

One more Big & Rich video
deserves a mention here, though it came a bit later in our career. It's the
video of the title song of our second album, **"Comin' to Your City."**
It opens with a grouchy old man (our dear friend Freddy Powers) sitting
and watching **"Save a Horse (Ride a Cowboy)"** on his TV and
grumbling, "Dang Big & Rich are a slap in the face of country music
with all that rock and roll." Then that old codger evaporates like he's
just been disintegrated with a space gun. The rest of the video takes
place in a guitar-shaped spaceship full of kick-ass hillbillies and other

BIG & RICH ON "COMIN' TO YOUR CITY"

JOHN: "Most expensive and craziest video we've ever done. What it might look like to ride around on magic mushrooms. Personified what we we're doing in 2006, coming to everybody's city."

BIG KENNY: "It's fun to space travel. It's a miniature version of being in a movie. We needed a spaceship to get to all those cities ..."

Kenny's journal, "Comin' to Your City" lyrics, June 9, 2003.

Behind the scenes
of the "Comin' to
Your City" video.

strange creatures as it travels from city to city, wreaking havoc. It's like an airborne version of the famed cantina scene from the original *Star Wars*. There are all kinds of extraterrestrial weirdos, including a green-headed monster that looks suspiciously like Two Foot Fred.

THE REAL BIG TIME

One way or another, through video, radio, and word of mouth, the word about us finally got out. The same week that the single of **"Save a Horse (Ride a Cowboy)"** peaked at number eleven on the country radio charts, the album that includes the song became the number one country album in America. We were, of course, blown away by this, especially because of the widely held belief, both inside the Nashville beltway and at many country radio stations, that Big & Rich was outside the box of commercial success. Big & Rich, many felt, didn't fit the mold and was therefore either unmarketable, or dangerous—or both. We proved them wrong, it appears, or maybe it's more to the point that the audience proved them wrong. By now we were just along for the ride.

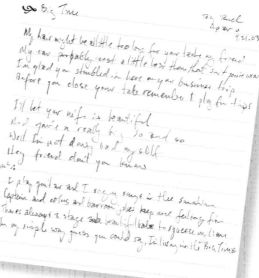

What all the early videos, particularly the "Save a Horse" musical extravaganza, announced about us was that we were singers and songwriters, for sure, but we were also, and maybe more so, a merry troupe of flat-out entertainers. We soon came to realize that our shared ambition was really twofold: first, to write and record some lasting songs, and second, to combine our talents and those of our traveling cast and crew into not just the greatest country music show in America, but no less than the greatest show on earth.

Lyrics to "Big Time," recorded in Big Kenny's journal on April 21, 2003.

Insane, you say? Probably, but hey, we shoot for the stars. We go for the hundred-to-one horse, not the two-to-one. And the pinnacle of that show is Big & Rich Live!

"Wish You Were Here!"

RIGHT: Big Kenny, the flower child, in Germany.

FAR RIGHT: John tames a wild mechanical pig in Germany.

BELOW: Embracing Vietnamese culture.

BELOW RIGHT: Hanging with the locals in Vietnam.

ABOVE: Taking in Chichén Itzá in Cancún, Mexico.

LEFT: John plays Trafalgar Square, London.

LEFT: Big Kenny visits Churchill's Tomb.

BELOW: Serenading the locals in London.

THIS PAGE: Posing with Big Ben.

WE'RE COMIN' TO YOUR CITY: THE BAND, THE CREW, THE ROAD

BIG KENNY: "I think we've finally gotten to the point where none of us put ourselves above the show. The show is the thing that's going to eventually put us at the top of everything."

JOHN: "Our fans, they show up at the concerts, that's for sure. A lot of acts with multiple number one hits—something we're still working on—join our show and open for us. Why? Because our fans are loyal and they buy tickets."

THE SHOW

It's all about the show.

Of all the things we do—recording, video, TV and radio appearances, and the rest—it's the live show that probably best defines who we are and what Big & Rich is all about. From the very beginning, we never wanted to simply go on a stage, politely sing our songs, take a bow, and leave. We wanted to put on a *show*. And we don't plan to stop until that show is greater than great.

John looks forward to the day we can bring a live African elephant on stage. Big Kenny looks forward to the day that we can shoot Two

Foot Fred out of a cannon. We're not kidding around here. We're coming to your city and we're going to give you a show you won't soon forget.

Come to one of our concerts and we'll try to give you what you might call a soul feeding. One of John's favorite tunes off our second record is the song **"Soul Shaker,"** full of manly, lover-boy pronouncements like

*"I'm gonna wrap you up in love like a hurricane
And blow you away."*

That's what we try to do every night on stage.

When people come to our shows, we want to jerk them from one emotional extreme to another, from **"Kick My Ass"** to **"Leap of Faith"** and back again. Every night we walk off the stage drained, like we've just been rode hard and put away wet, and the audience should feel pretty much the same. For those few hours, all of us—the musicians on stage and the fans in the cheap seats—are trying to live our lives to the fullest and have as much fun as we possibly can. The next morning you might wake up and discover, as John did, that your grandfather has terminal cancer, or some other personal tragedy in the making. You're liable to be blindsided at any point in this life; few people escape this sadness. Being at a concert like ours, if we are doing our job, is your respite from those dark moments. Just sing along with those idiots on stage and be thoroughly entertained.

SHOWTIME

Here's a recipe for a Big & Rich show. Start with four regular performers—the two of us plus Cowboy Troy and Two Foot Fred. Then add six stellar band members, headed up by Adam the Atomic Guitarist. To round out the roll call, there are at least twelve crew people who set up the stage and do everything from hanging backdrops and laying carpet to running a very complicated sound-and-light display. One guy, Steve Castro, does nothing but set up all the band gear (except the drums) and tune and maintain all twenty-five guitars used by us and the band. If Steve has a bad night, the whole band has a bad night.

We tour with four buses for people and two semis for the stuff. John likes to pull his Corvette in a trailer behind his bus so that he can make little side trips and get into trouble. Big Kenny likes to pull a trailer that

LEFT: Big Kenny, Atomic Adam, and John hanging out before a performance in Washington, DC.

ABOVE: Steve Castro tunes the guitars before a show.

Big Kenny on his bus with Jimmy Rector.

usually houses three of his motorcycles for the same reason. (He hauls three of them in case other people want to take a ride with him.) A lot of the fun on a Big & Rich tour happens before and after the show. Neither of us likes the idea of just going from bus to stage and back at every stop. Give us a few free minutes and we're off on some kind of adventure.

Big Kenny's bus is a great hangout space but also a home away from home for his wife and young son. There are baby beds and kids' toys

WHAT'S IN BIG KENNY'S CD PLAYER

1. Big & Rich 3
2. Damien Horne
3. *John Coltrane and Johnny Hartman*
4. *Queen—Greatest Hits*
5. Muse

WHAT'S IN JOHN'S CD PLAYER

1. *Frank Sinatra's Greatest Hits*
2. Aerosmith *Pump*
3. John Anderson *Easy Money*
4. *AC/DC Back in Black*
5. Ralph Stanley Gospel album

tossed around, like *Romper Room*. John's bus, on the other hand, is not particularly kid-friendly. Or eardrum- or headache-friendly, for that matter. It's got a state-of-the-art audio system, and the place is very, very loud. John likes to describe it as "a cross between Billy Bob's—the giant Texas honkytonk—and an underground techno bar."

John's bus is stocked with a world-class bar and a playlist of the most ridiculously eclectic music ever, much of it of the highly percussive sort. The bus thumps. It both thumps and rocks when there is a party on board, which is often. John's had thirty or forty people on his bus on a particularly spirited night. He invited a whole platoon of state troopers to join him on board one night in Illinois. There was a state trooper convention going on next door to the spot where we were playing. It was just the neighborly thing to do.

The portable Pub of Love.

Backstage, our intrepid tour manager, Shawn Pennington, is not only coordinating all of the above but also making sure we're all in the right mood to kick ass. Part of that involves something we built especially for the road—our own portable "Pub of Luv," a large road case that opens up into a fully stocked bar. Every night, it's the place where we all meet up before a show, check our ear monitors, warm up our guitar fingers,

ABOVE: Andy Hujdich, our wire guy.

OPPOSITE PAGE: John closes the show.

adjust our cowboy/top hats, and have one final toast before hitting the stage. We also return to this hallowed spot at the end of a show to high-five before we go back out for the encore.

You can take the boys out of the pub, but you can't take the pub out of the boys. It's just a bigger crowd, that's all, and they've actually paid money to hear us sing and play.

If you've been there, you know that the show is a *show*. For every performance, for instance, we spend a good six or seven thousand dollars solely on pyrotechnics—elaborate fireworks. That includes 175 or more individual explosions, big propane flame cannons, concussion blasts, and a mountain of streamers and confetti. It's like Dick Clark's *New Year's Rockin' Eve* every night. All we lack is the giant mirror ball descending in Times Square. Hey, maybe we'll add that on the next tour.

The whole event is a visual and sonic overload. Some country musicians strive to sound on stage like they sound on their albums—to give

Big Kenny greets a fan on Fremont Street in Las Vegas.

concertgoers the sense that they are hearing the actual recordings. That is not our goal. Our goal is to take the music and turn it into live, high-energy, multisensory theater. When we're cooking, we feel like some kind of nuclear fusion is happening between us. We explode. It's not just one plus one equals two out there. It's more like one plus one equals ten.

Unless you leave the concert with your ears ringing, your eyes wide open, and your body vibrating, then we haven't accomplished our mission.

Almost everything we do up on stage is an attempt to draw the audience in. When we're about to go into the song **"Big Time,"** for instance, we usually look for someone out in the crowd to bring on stage and sing along with us. It's his or her moment in the big time. Also, Big Kenny likes to give out a LOVE EVERYBODY guitar at each show, usually to a kid.

If we can get that old-time-revival feeling going, we are in for a good night. In fact, we mix some traditional elements of Southern gospel churchgoing right into the act. For example, ever since we started performing as a duo, we have stopped every show at a certain point to introduce the audience to one another. We say to everyone there, "Turn to your left or right, find someone you don't know, shake their hand, and introduce yourself." You could be meeting the love of your life, but you'll at least get a warm smile back and feel like you are all there to enjoy the show together. It's nothing but friendly, and creates a genuine communal atmosphere.

With Cowboy Troy on the set of the "Comin' to Your City" video.

That came right out of going to church every Sunday as kids. If a new person showed up at the service, we wanted to make him or her feel welcome. In a concert, it's just ten or twelve thousand new people making one another feel welcome.

"I'M COWBOY TROY, A TEXAS HICK . . ."

Then there's always the big moment when the six-foot, five-inch rapping cowboy, Cowboy Troy, joins us on stage to sing a couple of songs off his first album and get the crowd into a major dancing mood. Cowboy Troy can dance circles around all of us, and when he's center stage we just sit

back and watch him move. He usually ends his first song, "I Play Chicken with the Train," by standing on a platform as a blaze of fireworks comes shooting out of the end of his microphone.

To a lot of country music fans, seeing Troy up there for the first time is a shock. With very few exceptions, traditional country music is the music of white people, and some think it should be exclusively white music, which is as silly as saying R&B or rap music should be exclusively black. This association of country music with one race is a huge misconception perpetrated by a few prejudiced artists—very few—and a mass media that often inflates stereotypes rather than seeing beyond them. And it's also flat-ass not true.

"It's a simple fact: Music is color-blind."

It's a simple fact: *Music is color-blind*. Especially in America. The cross-fertilization of black and white and rural and urban music—from Motown to Willie, Waylon, and the boys—is what makes ours the dominant popular music on earth. We should be celebrating and expanding the mix of musical forms in this country, not trying to keep them in little race-based pigeonholes. We are only an extension of what country music has always been, from the blues songs of Hank Williams Sr. to the rock songs of Hank Williams Jr. As Hank Jr. would say, it's a family tradition.

Nevertheless, a guy like Troy singing country music is an affront to many traditional fans, and they can get ugly about it. We've seen Web sites where racists denounce Troy for denigrating country music and threaten him with bodily harm if he ever comes around to their part of America. Of course it escapes their demented view that Troy is *from*

OPPOSITE PAGE: Cowboy Troy in action.

BELOW: John and Cowboy Troy give it their all.

their part of America—Victoria, Texas, thank you—and is just as fond of country music as they are. Troy doesn't even like being called an "African American." As he likes to point out, he wasn't born in Africa, nor was his father, nor does he have any in-laws over there. He's just an American—a big tall one wearing a cowboy hat.

SHIFTING GEARS

Then it's Fred's turn. Fred is a guaranteed crowd pleaser. He usually opens the show and warms up the crowd with his own brand of Two Foot humor. Then he comes back on stage when it's time for the big finale number, **"Save a Horse (Ride a Cowboy),"** and usually a follow-up rendition of **"Rollin' (The Ballad of Big & Rich)."** We built a throne for him to sit on and chat it up before we begin the song. Then Fred gets into the groove, dancing and prancing around the stage, and his spirit is infectious. The peak of his performance is when he turns around and shakes his bootie for all the world to see. Fred is one awesome guy.

Eventually, we want to build a giant, spring-loaded jack-in-the-box that we can crank up and have Fred come popping up out the top. It's on the drawing boards, along with the cannon-shooting stunt. The sky's the limit when it comes to Two Foot Fred on stage.

Fred helps us entertain the crowd.

Then there are special moments in the show that have grown out of the songs themselves and radically shift the whole mood. We love to direct attention to others while on stage, especially those neglected or suffering, whether it's women caught in abusive relationships (**"Holy Water"**), or maybe the victims of the horror going on in the Darfur region of Sudan in Africa where they use rape as a weapon of war, or a whole gen-

LADIES AND GENTLEMEN, MR. TWO FOOT FRED!

"... Good evening everyone and welcome to the Big & Rich show! I'm Two Foot Fred, the Ambassador of Attractions for Big & Rich, and I'm here to get you all pumped up!

"... You know, the other day I was sitting in a park smoking a really great cigar. This guy walks up and says, 'Hey, little man, don't you know cigars will stunt your growth?' So I say, 'Where were you twenty years ago?'

"... Does anybody in here like roller coasters? Well, I don't. They've got that sign that says you must be forty-two inches to ride! All I know is *thank God* my last girlfriend didn't have that rule!

"... You know, I get to meet a lot of people in the music business. Last week I met Miss Dolly Parton. She gave me a great big hug and now I know the true meaning of *Dollywood!*

"... I used to think I was the shortest man in country music, until I met Kenny Chesney.

"... Ready for the show? Well, here they are ... *Big & Rich!*"

Fred doing warm-up act.

eration of Vietnam veterans who are just beginning to be thanked by the nation for their service (**"8th of November"**). We'll talk about those concerns later in the book, but when we bring them up nightly as part of our live show, we're not out to preach and we're certainly not out to promote a political agenda. The idea is simply to shine a light on a problem and let the audience at least know that these are some of the things we think about every day.

**ABOVE TOP:
Our production
manager and
monitor engineer,
Curt Jenkins.**

ABOVE: Assistant
tour manager
Steve Schweidel
borrows Big
Kenny's top hat.

The stage ritual around the nightly performance of "8th of November," perhaps a high-water mark for us so far, is pretty set by now. We play the opening to the video by Kris Kristofferson as a way of explaining the origin of the song and our involvement in the whole campaign to recognize the contributions of soldiers from the Vietnam era. Then we usually invite some of those vets on stage with us, along with a color guard holding the American flag. That always gets the crowd on its feet. Then Big Kenny leads the audience into the Pledge of Allegiance, we give a final salute to the soldiers, and they exit the stage.

"Holy Water" has now become a kind of tribute song in the show for anyone out there in need of love and compassion. It's usually the point in the show where we show a banner reading SAVE DARFUR and briefly talk about the situation over there. It's not a long dissertation, for sure, not a lesson in North African politics or international relations. It's just a simple reminder that we now live in a global village and are inevitably drawn into people's lives around the world. Given the fact that you can turn on CNN and be connected to anywhere on earth, our music has grown into country music without *geographic* prejudice, too.

In a way, songs like "8th of November" and "Holy Water," and the moments they create on stage, are a direct antithesis to the rowdy, good-time music of "Save a Horse (Ride a Cowboy)" and "Comin' to Your City." It's the other side of the coin, the yin to the yang (there's that concept again). It's also a distinctive element of what we do, and will continue to do. We've had the great good fortune to be given this big stage, so to speak, to express ourselves to the world—and we mean everyone, not just the rock-till-you-drop folks. In our minds, it's all good and it's all country music.

After ninety minutes of this emotional and sensory roller coaster, we're wiped out. John says that he knows he's had a good time, and probably the crowd, too, if he has a splitting headache, his ears are ringing, he feels a stabbing pain in his rib cage, his knees feel like they're going to buckle, and he can't catch his breath. It's as if we've just played a hard-fought football game or maybe run a marathon—we're beat up and elated. It usually takes us a few minutes to lick a wound or two and regain our equilibrium, but the afterglow is like nothing else on earth.

Martin Frey, front-of-house engineer.

LIVING ON THE ROAD

We not only do a big show, we do a lot of them. In 2006, we had more than a hundred full-blown concert performances. This included as many benefit performances as we could squeeze in, from Katrina relief to colorectal cancer research. After less than four years on the road, we were already headlining almost every show we played, but we also went

Marc Oswald and Big Kenny hit the road.

out with major headliners like Kenny Chesney, Tim McGraw, and Brooks & Dunn who can fill stadiums. At the County Fest in Cadott, Wisconsin, last year, we played to a record-breaking crowd of forty-seven thousand kindred souls. It's a trip, of course, whether we're playing for a bunch of neighbors in a local charity event or a sea of neighbors in a local arena.

In addition to performances last year, we visited ninety or more radio stations as part of an ongoing radio tour, did dozens of TV and award show appearances, and played more than our share of small bars late into the night. That adds up to a lot of time on the road. By the end of 2006, we'd hit something like 250 cities across America.

There are a lot of ways to break up the monotony of long drives and constant work, and they don't all involve drinking. One surefire tactic is to venture out from the venue and see what's going on in the local surroundings. John has his Corvette to drive around, and Big Kenny has his Harleys. If there is enough time, Big Kenny and a couple of bike-riding buddies might take off for the mountains, ride into the wilderness, and sit on a mountaintop and breathe. John will most likely hop in his 'Vette, tune in Frank Sinatra, punch the ON STAR button, and hear back, "Hello, Mr. Rich, what can we do for you today?" John then has them run down a list of the most appealing attractions—bowling alleys or "Bob's Beer Barn" or nightclub/honky-tonks—in the area. He picks one or two and checks them out. This inevitably leads to trouble later that evening.

About once a year, John will drive around looking for a used-car lot to buy a vehicle to give away. The last time he did this was in Nebraska while we were playing a big fairgrounds. John found the right dealer and the right vehicle—a used Ford pickup for about fifteen hundred bucks. He told the salesman he'd buy the truck if the guy would drive it over to the fairgrounds. When the dealer finally figured out who John was, he was thrilled to do it.

That night at the show, the truck was proudly situated next to the stage. It had been autographed by us and the whole crew and filled with all kinds of Big & Rich merchandise and music. We also rigged it with a ton of pyro to blow up at the appropriate time. John then announced early in the show that one of our lucky female fans would be getting the keys to this **"brand-new used 1991 Ford F-150 with 250,000 miles on it"** if she can prove to him that she's the single most enthusiastic female Big & Rich fan in the audience tonight.

Needless to say, a lot of enthusiastic females jump up and down and scream and shout and dance and strut and do anything they can think of short of public nudity to get that prize. Finally, John picks one hysterical lass and hands her the keys. As she descends upon her new truck, the pyro-and-light show goes off and the lucky lady drives off in her truck for the ages.

THE SHOW AFTER THE SHOW

On many, many occasions when we're on the road, the show doesn't end when we sing our last encore on stage. It often just moves to a different, more intimate location in the surrounding area. We'll be playing a show in front of twenty thousand or so rabid fans and then announce on our way off stage that John has located a very nice watering hole in the community and if anyone wants to join us there, we might be persuaded to sing a few beer-hall tunes. We usually don't end up drinking alone.

Fred remembers when we were doing a big show at the Clio Amphitheatre in Clio, Michigan. John had unloaded the 'Vette and was doing what came naturally to him: tooling around town, looking for an after-party locale. He found the perfect little twelve-lane bowling alley with a full bar—Clio Bowling Arcade—and designated it Party Central. After we announced on stage that we were going to be there, a couple thousand of our closest friends showed up to greet us.

In Fred's words, "We just blew that place up." We ended up renting every single lane in the joint and treating our friends to a night of free bowling. We threw bowling contests where the first topless person to roll a strike won a thousand bucks. We bought rounds of Crown Royal by the carload and jammed on stage with Fred, Troy, Adam the Atomic Guitarist, and a few other stragglers. It was like a Mafia night at a bowling alley instead of the Pub of Luv. And it was a story for those two thousand people to tell for years to come.

Sometimes we'll pull into some town and create a party even if we aren't doing a major concert. Last summer, between concerts, we were on a radio tour in the Northeast. A radio tour involves visiting big radio stations in major markets and often playing a song or two on the air, live. One day we were driving through New York State, having just hit three stations that day, and were approaching the town of Binghamton when we asked our radio promotions guy, Jimmy Rector, if there was a station nearby. He said yes, and he even knew the manager. Ready to blow off a little extra steam, we said, "Well, let's drop in unannounced and see what happens."

So we knock on the station door and Jimmy's buddy answers at the same time he's broadcasting on the air (it was a little station). We cheerfully march in and take over. For the next hour and a half, we are on the air, live, playing songs and acting up. Along the way, John decides that we should stage a makeout contest. He tells people to come down to the station to make out, then decides we should find a bar for this event. The radio guy calls a friend and talks him into opening his tavern, though the whole staff is off playing a softball game. John tells the radio audience that if someone will bring the lobster and crab cakes, we'll head down to the bar and perform.

Forty-five minutes later, we pull up to this bar in our buses—and there are twelve hundred people outside ready to get in and make out. Grandmas and little kids are all part of the crowd—it's a family affair. John ends up both emceeing and being the professional kisser in the makeout contest, and Jimmy, our bus driver Stewart Holdsworth, and

ABOVE TOP: Big Kenny, Gary Sinise, and John Rich at a benefit for veterans in Washington, DC.

ABOVE: John Rich, Lee Ann Womack, and Big Kenny.

With Cowboy Troy at ESPN *GameDay.*

Big Kenny are the judges. We pick the ten prettiest contestants and pick the winner. It's a tough job.

The bar tab was over ten thousand dollars. It was worth every penny.

Someday we would like to combine the stage show and the after-stage show into one long acoustical tour. It would be just the two of us—no fireworks, no Two Foot Fred—with a couple of acoustic guitars, a couple of chairs, and a couple of microphones. We wouldn't call the tour "Big & Rich." We'd call it the "John and Kenny tour." We'd pull into a bar or a small club near you, set up on stage, and proceed to play whatever the hell came to mind. It would be a return to those early Muzik Mafia days where you just made it up as you went along. When that works, it is about as much fun as you can have playing music.

ROLLIN' ON THE CMAS

Big Kenny and John Rich with G. Gordon Liddy.

The live show and the success of *Horse of a Different Color* led to a genuine milestone: an appearance on the Country Music Awards. Our

very first live performance on the CMAs was an honor and a thrill, but it was also filled with some serious high drama. The executive producer of the show, the legendary Walter Miller, had asked us to appear and specifically requested that we perform **"Rollin' (The Ballad of Big & Rich)."** We hadn't even released the song as a single, but Walter thought it had an important message to convey. Plus, he wanted to see the black rapping cowboy on stage with us, a historic moment not just for the CMAs but for country music, period. We were beyond excited, both for the chance to perform with Troy and the fact that we had been nominated for that year's Horizon Award for Best New Artist. (In the end, we got beaten out by some upstart named Gretchen Wilson.)

There was just one small hitch—a hitch in Kenny's neck. Because of that car wreck many years before, Kenny suffered from chronic neck and back pain, and in the days leading up to the CMA broadcast, the pain was killing him. The morning of the show, he went to his doctor to get an injection to relieve the pain and inflammation. Right after the shot, his left arm became completely paralyzed. It just stopped working. Kenny couldn't move it, let alone play a guitar or even hold a mike. The doctor assured him that the paralysis was temporary and would be gone by showtime, showtime only being about eight hours ahead.

Needless to say, everybody involved, from Walter Miller to John Rich—especially John—was freaked about this. Kenny had to miss the last big dress rehearsal at noon before the live show that evening. John thought of rounding up a big cardboard cutout of Kenny to stick up on stage in case Kenny couldn't make it. And Kenny had only one functioning arm.

While John and the others worried about what-if, Kenny went home and slept all day. At around four in the afternoon, his then girlfriend, Christiev, woke him and more or less shoved him into a limo to be driven to the ceremony and the walk on the red carpet. The doctor, it turned out, was right on the mark—the arm sprang back into action just in the nick of time. Barely two hours after waking up, Kenny stood right up there on stage next to John, Troy, and Fred and sang and played his heart out. "I present to you," he shouted, "country music without prejudice!"

As we sang and Troy danced and rapped, the audience looked a bit stunned. They knew that this CMA-sanctioned country performance with fiddles, guitars, multiple rock licks, and Cowboy Troy was delivering a nationwide message: Country music is moving forward. In retrospect, it was a huge night for both of us—a kind of public acknowledgment we had dreamed of since the early days of the Muzik Mafa. To think, given the lingering consequences of a random car accident of years past, it almost didn't happen.

THE GRAND OLE OPRY

We have had our share of television performances: our career-launching performance of **"Save a Horse (Ride a Cowboy)"** on the ACMs in 2004, *The Tonight Show with Jay Leno, Good Morning America,* and *Imus,* plus special performances that run the gamut from commemorating a Vietnam War memorial in South Dakota to singing a reworked version of **"Comin' to Your City"** as the theme song for ESPN's *College GameDay.* Probably the most special of special performances, certainly for John's family, came when we were invited to play at the Grand Ole Opry last summer. This was a first, unprecedented both for the Opry people and for us.

The Grand Ole Opry is no doubt the most traditional organization in country music. It is the embodiment of the history of the music dating back to its first radio broadcast as the *WSM Barn Dance* in November 1925, more than eighty years ago. For the Opry folks to invite Big & Rich to perform on their stage—along with a total country anomaly like Cowboy Troy—was to us a testament to how far our careers had come and how the most traditional forum now saw us as legitimate members of the country music community. Even a year earlier, this would not have happened. And a six-foot, five-inch black cowboy performing rap music? That had *never* happened.

As a way to honor this very special event in our lives, we took the song **"Save a Horse (Ride a Cowboy)"** and changed it musically into a country swing song in the tradition of the great Bob Wills and His Texas Playboys. We then performed it along with the in-house Grand Ole Opry band, a group of dyed-in-the-wool country traditionalists. This was our way of tipping our hat back to the great Opry legacy and the respect in which we held the tradition they were keeping alive.

John's father, a lover of the Opry since back in the days when it was the absolute center of the country music universe, came to that show along with assorted grandparents and other in-laws. As we mentioned earlier, John's dad had his own dreams as a young man of a life in country music—and in his day, especially, that dream hinged on making a breakout appearance on the Opry stage.

The Opry now tapes two shows in one evening, separated by a two-

Jim and John Rich perform at the Grand Ole Opry.

Big Kenny and
little Lincoln.

hour break. While John was eating with his family during the downtime, he turned to his dad and said, **"You know, one of these days you're going to have get up on the stage of the Opry and sing with me."**

His dad replied, "Well, you know me, son, I'm good for it anytime you are."

And John said, **"You know what ... would you want to do it tonight?"** His dad looked at him in shock and said, "You mean, like in an hour? You think they'd let me?"

John called Pete Fisher, general manager of the Opry, and before you could say *Little Jimmy Dickens*, John and his dad were on stage rehearsing for their big number. The song they chose to perform together was the Tennessee Ernie Ford classic "Sixteen Tons." It was one of the first songs John's dad had ever taught him, and in fact one of the first songs his dad had ever learned to play and sing himself.

So, in the middle of the second show, John brought his dad out on stage, introduced him, and together they sang "Sixteen Tons." When the song ended, his dad got a standing ovation. It was a forty-year-old dream that had finally, magically, come true.

FRED ACTS UP

Fred has a favorite television story that he loves to tell to anyone who will listen. It occured during an appearance on *Jimmy Kimmel Live* on ABC during our first summer of touring after the debut of **"Save a Horse (Ride a Cowboy)."** Jimmy had been on a Super Bowl show earlier that year where he did a football skit using little people as pro football players. At the end of the skit, he turned to the audience and said, "Wasn't that great? Midgets are cool. Everyone should own one."

Fred hates the term *midget*, and figured he needed to bust Jimmy's chops for such a surly attitude toward little people. So when we get the call to appear on Jimmy's late-night show, Fred told us the story of the Super Bowl putdown and insisted on joining us on stage. We of course said, "By all means."

When Fred hit the stage to join us in "Save a Horse," he was wearing a T-shirt he had made up that proudly announced: KIMMEL CAN KISS MY ASS. In the interview segment after the song, Jimmy approached Fred and asked, "So what's this T-shirt all about?"

"Jimmy . . . karma. It's all about karma," Fred replied curtly.

Kimmel, sensing a comic duel in the making, asked Fred, "Hey, little man, do you even have an ass?"

"Sure do," Fred answered, and proceeded to turn around, bend over, and stick it in Jimmy's face.

It was all in jest, of course, but there is a moral here: Don't be calling Fred a midget or in any way demeaning his stature. You're liable to get the Jimmy Kimmel treatment.

THE SHOW OF THE FUTURE

We've been on the road performing as Big & Rich for about four years. It seems like a lifetime to us, but compared with the careers of other long-standing country stars, it's not much time at all. What will our live show look like four, five, six years from now? Probably a whole lot different. It's an ever-changing organism. We keep adding elements like the **"8th of November"** tribute we now do in every show, and keep imagining elements we'd like to add.

Remember, we're shooting for the greatest show on earth. To that end, we're looking around right now for a world-class illusionist to join the show and wow the audience with some mind-bending sleight of hand. The next time you see us, we may appear out of thin air in a puff of smoke to open the show, or be levitated out over the crowd, just for the hell of it. John has his elephant act that he's working on. To add even more wondrous sideshow elements, it may be time to call in some stone pros like the people at the world-famous Barnum & Bailey Circus.

As the showman once said, "You ain't seen nothing yet!"

Meet the Band

✳

FAR LEFT:
Electric guitar/
bandleader:
Adam "The
Atomic Guitarist"
Shoenfeld.

MIDDLE LEFT:
Pedal steel/
mandolin/piddle:
James "Uncle
Penn"
Pennebaker.

LEFT: Piano/
keyboards: Jeff
Armstrong.

FAR LEFT: Bass:
Ethan "Easy"
Pilzer.

MIDDLE LEFT:
Drums: Larry
Babb.

LEFT: The Band,
2006.

THE FREAK PARADE FANS

BIG KENNY: "Our fans are freakish. They just travel around. There are people that you will see at maybee fifteen, twenty shows a year. They are avid. And they help us to do great things."

JOHN: "As just a show of respect, you know, they'll show up wearing rhinestone Wranglers or a big top hat or whatever. I've heard some artists say about their own fanatical fans, 'What is wrong with these people?' I say, they're just into it. They aren't trying to look like me or Big Kenny all the time; they're just part of the show . . . "

THE FREAK PARADE

Welcome to the Freak Parade.

Our music grew in popularity through a number of channels, including country radio, music videos, and mass media. Many of our fans more or less found us by word of mouth, seeing us initially on tour with Tim McGraw, or maybe through an extra-musical news item about Darfur or our work with Vietnam vets. However they came to find us, once they found us, they—you—have remained steadfast,

Playing for the Freak Parade members at the first official fan club party in Nashville.

loyal, and just a little crazy. Okay, at times real crazy, but that's why we love you. You give us back as much as or more than we give you.

Eclectic country music produces an eclectic crowd of listeners and supporters, one that's impossible to define in easy terms like *young, old, conservative, out of control,* or *white suburban males between the ages of fifteen and thirty-four.* We stand on stage and look out at the crowd, and we see a highly diverse bunch of people. We see a guy in the middle of the auditorium with spiked hair and nose rings with his arm around a girlfriend in head-to-toe tattoos, dressed like a Goth. They're probably not there as a lark—they scream out the words to the songs right along with everyone else. Right next to them is a big ol' country boy wearing a LYNYRD SKYNYRD T-shirt with his arm around a girl wearing Wranglers, a big belt buckle, and a REDNECK WOMAN baseball cap.

When it's time to stop the show and meet your neighbor, the Goth and the cowboy shake hands and smile like they just saw each other in church that morning. Or the Goth turns the other way to shake hands with a guy dressed exactly like Big Kenny—big hat and a T-shirt reading LOVE EVERYBODY—and he's holding up a big sign reading I'M NOT AFRAID.

"Follow the bouncing ball . . ."

Follow the bouncing ball: "Somebody's got to be unafraid to lead the Freak Parade." That's the line, repeated a dozen times, that opens our second album, *Comin' to Your City.* It is a direct call to our fans to carry on. By the time we released this record, we were already very familiar with the people who frequented our shows. They were single moms touched by **"Holy Water,"** working guys and their girlfriends out for a little **"Save a Horse (Ride a Cowboy)"** fun, gray-haired veterans wearing 173RD AIRBORNE bomber jackets, or teenagers who were at a Kid Rock concert the weekend before and headed toward a Merle Haggard concert the next night. It would be overstating it to say they were a cross section of America, but they are a rich mix of many different kinds of Americans—a mix we hope will get richer as time goes on.

Increasingly, as we survey the crowd, it's also starting to look a little peppered out there, an array of races and cultures brought together under one musical tent. Bottom line, this is one of the main things we want to accomplish with our music—break down barriers.

The rhythmic and lyrical extremes in the second album, *Comin' to Your City*—befitting our newfound assurance that we weren't the only freaks is town—are greater even than our debut album. It goes from **"Soul Shaker"**—

"You're so fine you'd make a bulldog break his chain
I'm gonna wrap you up in love like a hurricane"

—to a somber requiem about a horrendous war battle that took place in Indochina on November 8, 1965. In between are pop-tinged ballads like **"Never Mind Me"** and **"Blow My Mind,"** and even a little nose thumbing at the **"Filthy Rich."**

Gretchen Wilson, Big Kenny, Kid Rock, and John Rich at Kid Rock's sold-out concert at the Arena in Chattanooga, 2004.

We ended *Comin' to Your City* with our own anthem about America: "The Star Spangled Banner" interwoven with "The Pledge of Allegiance" and excerpts from the Declaration of Independence and Martin Luther King Jr.'s "I Have a Dream" speech. Joining us are Cowboy Troy and Gretchen Wilson. Especially after our experience with the Vietnam vets of **"8th of November,"** not to mention the thousands of soldiers being killed and maimed in Iraq and Afghanistan, we thought it was important to remind people where exactly they lived.

Big Kenny recites the Pledge of Allegiance.

REPEAT OFFENDERS

We have no statistics to offer, but when we stand in line and greet fans before a show or simply look out at an audience as we perform, we see a lot of repeat offenders. We see people in Milwaukee whom we saw two weeks earlier in Des Moines or Indianapolis. When we have a chance to chat with these avid camp followers, they tell us that they find a show and location every month and come see us. It's their hobby, and they pursue it with a passion. Some people spend their weekends running marathons or hitting the backwoods in their ATVs. The hard-core Freak Paraders spend their weekends celebrating with us and twelve thousand soul mates of the brotherhood of freakdom.

We always hoped that our fans would get into the music like we do on stage, but we never figured they would be so . . . fanatical. They are completely engaged. They don't just stand for one song, then tune out and play footsie with their girlfriend. They are standing up the minute we walk on stage and they never sit down. It's like the most enthusiastic gospel revival on earth.

The freakier fans go a step farther—they start dressing like us. We consider it the ultimate show of respect, although it can be a little unnerving to look out at a crowd and see three or four people have your black-on-black cowboy look down to a T, or spot a couple of dozen people wearing top hats. Even little kids. Someone spent a serious amount of time stitching together a hat that's the spitting image of Big Kenny's. And over the course of a tour, we see hundreds of them.

One of our all-time-favorite look-alike moments is the time when Fred and his brother Toby became the three-foot version of Big & Rich. Toby is Big Kenny and Fred is John. Fred has the right jeans and a mustache cut exactly like John's, and Toby is wearing a bushy-looking wig, a top hat, and a LOVE EVERYBODY sleeveless T-shirt.

TROUBLE

Two Foot Fred knows our fans probably better than we do. We are connected to them through their mail and brief backstage meet-and-greet encounters, but Fred is out there every night working the crowd and meeting the people, especially those who come to multiple shows.

One man Fred has told us about is nicknamed "Trouble." Trouble— aka David Boone—is a thirteen-year-old and he lives in the Baltimore area. He suffers from cerebral palsy due to a premature birth and has spent his brief life in a wheelchair. Nevertheless, he loves his country music. According to Fred, Trouble has been to at least fifty Tim McGraw concerts. In fact, it was Tim, according to Trouble, who gave him the nickname in the first place.

Trouble caught us at one of Tim's shows and became an ardent supporter. He saw us first in Virginia Beach in 2004 and has now been to fourteen B&R concerts. When asked why he liked our show so much, Trouble got right to the point. "Because with them," he said, "being different doesn't matter. They are different and fun!"

Hanging out with fans at CMA Fest 2006.

Fred likes to say that he "converted" Trouble into a Big & Rich fan—no, Fred, it was the music—but in any case, Trouble and Fred have struck up a lasting friendship. When Trouble comes to a show, he rings Fred up on his cell phone and they hang out. Fred has an infectious, can-do spirit, and apparently this has rubbed off on Trouble. Fred is not only the Ambassador of Attractions. He's also the Ambassador of Determination, and guys like Trouble can see this much better than the rest of us.

Another fan Fred likes to talk about is Matt Chang, who may hold the dubious honor of being our biggest fan. He's in his midtwenties, lives in Washington, DC, and works at the US Department of State as a Diplomatic Security Officer. It's amazing that he can even hold down a job, given the amount of time he's spent following us around. You never know where Matt might appear. Since his first Big & Rich concert at WMZQ Fest on May 7th, 2004 in Bristow, Virginia, we've seen him at more concerts than we can count. We've also seen him at the Muzik Mafia events in Nashville and even at an ABC *Good Morning America* taping in New York City. Keep it up, Matt, and you might end up on stage someday!

Then there's Paul Wright, chat room handle PawPaw. Paul is a big fifty-year-old biker dude with a ponytail and a body covered with tattoos. When he's not working his day job at a cable communications contracting firm, he's likely chasing us down. He's logged seventeen shows so far, from California to Florida. PawPaw is a well-known figure in the Big & Rich world—he calls himself "a Muzik Mafia Soldier for life"—and he is as different from Matt as Matt is from Trouble. But like Trouble said, we couldn't care less. They are all lovable freaks to us.

On the official Freak Parade bulletin boards—go to www.freak parade.com—there is a whole world going on. Hard-core parader Kellydew (aka Kelly Dewey), for instance, posted over 500 times in three months last year. Fans dig deep into why our music is so important to them, and they are all over our comings and goings. They often know our tour dates before they've even been announced! And the fans don't need us to have a good time. At a recent Las Vegas fan club get-together, the fans had their own party before the official party with us.

THE NEW PARROTHEADS

The Big & Rich Freak Parade, in our minds, is increasingly becoming the country music version of Jimmy Buffett's Parrotheads or—the granddaddy of all die-hard fan groups—the Grateful Dead's Deadheads. When fans become as avid and dedicated as ours, they cease to be just fans and become almost a community of like-minded souls. They start seeing one another at concerts, which leads to e-mail exchanges, which leads to activities over and above just singing along to **"Save a Horse (Ride a Cowboy)."** A dedicated fan community takes on a life of its own. We're just here to rally them to the cause.

Big Kenny wrote a song that tries to sum up our experience of the people who come to see us and give us so much energy and good feeling. It's called **"It's a Lot Like Woodstock."** The song describes the images we see in front of us:

"Baseball caps and big top hats and lighters lighting up the sky / Pig tails, ponytails, fat-bottomed girls, dancing to the bump and grind . . ."

It also describes the sheer movement we see:

"Boogie, boogie, boogie, fiddlin', groovin', fist just a pumpin', hands a wavin' high, start jumpin' . . ."

That person you shake hands with, the song says, just might turn out to be

"the love of your life, it's a lot like Woodstock."

And that's not our fantasy of the audience. That's the audience. When we play big summer festivals where people have more than one

John Rich displays this photo of himself and Loretta Lynn in his home.

night to let themselves go, it can turn into a Big & Rich World. Much like a NASCAR weekend, they line up their campers, build their own on-the-spot discos and karaoke bars, and start the party a day or two before we even show up. They're already donning their top hats and rhinestone Wranglers and handmade I'M NOT AFRAID T-shirts and just waiting for *us* to join *their* party.

And that's what it comes down to, really. The Freak Parade is not just *at* the show, cheering us on. The Freak Parade is *part* of the show, and we hope they'll stay part of the show for years and years to come.

FREAKPARADE.COM

Freak Parade is not only the name of our fans, it's the name of our official fan club. Only a little over a year old as we write, the club is already full of die-hard members and growing rapidly. Most of these hard-core Freak Paraders are from the United States, but they extend all the way to Australia, the UK, and even our soldiers in Iraq. The oldest official

member was born in 1934 and the youngest, in 1993. A lot of members are not from the South, the traditional bastion of country music. They're from Pennsylvania, Minnesota, and New Jersey, not to mention all the other forty-seven states. In other words, they are from the whole *country*.

Where is the Freak Parade headed? Taking a page from the Parrotheads, we hope to rally the troops to go beyond partying to raising awareness, fixing problems, and venturing out into the community on a global scale. Wouldn't it be cool to see all the Freak Paraders aligned with all the Mafia soldiers, marching down Fifth Avenue in New York to bring attention to the horror of Darfur? Maybe we should get to work on that parade permit.

How I Discovered Big & Rich

Fans Share Their Stories

Melanie Shirley

The past several years I had been in a kind of slow depressing slump and headed downward. Hating my job, life, etc. An old high school friend brought me a copy of *HOADC* in May '04. As I started wearing that CD out, in the car, all day at work, I started getting healthy, exercising, losing weight, etc. All the newfound music gave me new life.

By November '04 I had lost enough weight that I had the confidence to attend my 20 yr high school reunion. Attending that is what led me to meet my husband. We married August of this year '06. Mind you I met him at a pub in my hometown after the reunion where I was having a "Big Time" and getting the dj to play B&R and Gretchen Wilson. That is what caught his attention to me. I knew if he liked that music, we would surely get along.

So in short you changed my life, my attitude, opened up a whole new muzikal world that has included some great travels to see them and meet wonderful friends, and meet my husband.

Jean Day

Being older than y'all, I was raised more "Victorian." When I first heard "SAHRAC," I thought "this is going too far." I didn't like them and was not going to listen to them. I normally work with CMT playing so in May 2005 I heard a beautiful song, ran in to hear it. It was "Holy Water." You could see the compassion and love so clearly in Kenny and John's faces. My younger sister Sandra was murdered in cold blood by her husband after being abused for many years. It is a tragedy you never get over, ever. I could feel they really cared.

It happened that they were coming to Cherokee 5/28. Sharon and I went to see them. I was astounded. Their music made me feel young and so happy and when Kenny held out both hands to me and I somehow got past the security guard it was like an electric shock (probably pyrotechnics but still not sure). That did it. Next day I bought their CDs, DVDs, anything that said Big & Rich. Listen to them *EVERY* day, if I feel really down or even sick, just hearing their voices is a magic cure.

Lorenda Sue Patterson

My son, now age 14, was the one who got me into Big & Rich, due to his love of a certain song about a cowboy and a horse. From my searching to find out more about these gentlemen, I came to enjoy their music as well. There's one particular instance involving Big & Rich and my son that always brings a smile.

Middle-school age boys can be fun to be around, but sometimes have a mood that only they can comprehend. One day when I picked my son up from school he was in one of those incomprehensible moods. I believe it was during the fall of 2004. I was playing the radio on my preferred station and Alan Jackson's song "Little Bitty" was playing as my son got in the car. When my son hears the "it's alright to be little bitty" line, he immediately hits the button on the stereo to play the CD (which was *Horse of a Different Color*!) and states "it's not alright to be little bitty, you've got to be big and rich!"

We listened to Big & Rich all the way home that day.

Catherine Pavao

I recently lost my Husband unexpectedly . . . A devastating life change for me . . . We were so much in love & had this wonderful life ahead of us . . . all ripped away in a matter of seconds . . . it is so hard, so very hard for me to try to live with . . . there are times I hardly make it thru the day . . . we have five children, Penny 24, Joey, 22, Chantelle, 20, Joshua 16 & Corinne 13 & a grandson, Jared.

I have been a Big & Rich fan from the first time I heard "Wild West Show" years back . . . Me and my Husband heard that song for the first time while we were together on vacation in North Conway, New Hampshire . . . we went to the local Wal-Mart and bought our first Big & Rich CD, of course from there I was hooked . . . Unknowingly to Big Kenny and John Rich they have gotten me thru a personal heartache that no one should have to endure . . . the loss of my husband this past April without warning has been unbearable.

One of the harsh realities for me has been trying to listen to the radio . . . I avoided it . . . at all costs . . . this is where Kenny and John come in . . . thru out the summer their music has been all I could listen to . . . along with my children . . . They have gotten me thru some of the lowest moments of my life and have brought back a smile to my face and laughter when I have been at a place were the heartache is beyond explanation . . . so many times over and over again . . . Thank You . . . from the bottom of my heart . . . I have so much gratitude for the two of you . . . Sincere Thanks from deep within . . . Cathy & Mario P & our Children . . . Penny, Joey, Chantelle, Josh and Corinne & our grandson Baby Jared.

Brent and Gina Rice
Our story begins back in 2004 on our way to Lame Deer, Montana, leading a mission group to the Cheyenne Indian Reservation. As we were leading a caravan of people from Indiana my daughter (Chelsea) saw a bumper sticker that said "Save a Horse, Ride a Cowboy." My daughter got a kick out of that and then my husband said "Hey that is a song—from the parade group or something." On the long ride we finally heard the song and fell in love with it. We made a stop at Wal-Mart in Rapid City, S.D. to pick up supplies before we got onto the reservation so my daughter purchased the CD for her step-dad.

We all love the song "Wild West Show" because of what we are doing on the reservation. We are building a youth camp for the Cheyenne, Crow and American people. This song talks about putting our difference aside and learning from each other. We went on our 1st mission trip in 1999 and it changed our lives forever. We have since started a not for profit and we are bringing others to the reservation to help build the camp and to learn from each other. We have personally adopted the song "Wild West Show" as our theme.

B&R has touched our lives in many ways. Through our mission trips, vacations, and giving Brent and I something to do together. They have truly made an impact on our life.

8TH OF NOVEMBER: BIG & RICH FROM THE HEART

BIG KENNY: "When I was five years old, I thought I was going to probably be a preacher, an electrician, or a fireman. Those were the things I thought about. I completely cut my musical teeth in church. That was the only place where I sang aloud in a crowd."

JOHN: "My dad is a preacher. I'm not a preacher, Big Kenny's not a preacher, but our music preaches to a certain level. Whether it's preaching to people to go out and have a real great time or it's preaching about veterans or holy water, whatever it is, it allows us to speak out. Some kind of evangelistic DNA is in both of us."

NILES HARRIS

On Monday morning, November 8, 1965, the United States was just beginning a long, frustrating, and ultimately disheartening war with Communist forces in South Vietnam. Niles Harris was a nineteen-year-old Midwestern boy turned infantryman and parachutist (or

Big Kenny, Niles Harris, and John Rich in War Zone D, Hill 65, Vietnam.

"sky soldier") with the 173rd Airborne Brigade. After traveling to Vietnam this past year, it was apparent to us that our American soldiers had planted seeds of democracy that are beginning to blossom some forty years later.

The 173rd is an infantry unit capable of parachuting into a war zone if necessary. Created in 1963, it was the very first combat unit to go to Vietnam, arriving in May 1965. On November 8, Niles was in a lead platoon on a search-and-destroy mission in a thick jungle area called Hill 65 in War Zone D. They were ready to engage the enemy. Unfortunately, the enemy that day was a force of twelve hundred Vietcong soldiers. It was a massacre. Out of all the 173rd soldiers caught up in this ambush, forty-eight were killed. Of the thirty men in Harris's platoon, only five survived. Other forces came to the rescue of Niles and the other wounded, dragging them back to safety.

Niles suffered severe injuries to his legs that kept him in army hospitals for the next two years. He got through his injuries and came back to do three more tours of duty in Vietnam; he eventually retired after twenty-five years of special forces service. For his bravery that day, he received the Purple Heart. As Big Kenny would later quip, Niles was a pretty decent bartender but he was a damn good soldier.

"Niles was a pretty decent bartender but he was a damn good soldier."

✳

In that same battle of November 8, a black medic named Lawrence Joel, also wounded in combat, endangered his life many times over to save as many of his comrades as he could. For this, he became the first living African American since the Spanish-American War to be awarded the United States Medal of Honor. The 173rd Airborne continued to be deployed throughout the 1960s; it was deactivated in 1972, then reactivated for duty in both Iraq and Afghanistan.

After serving his country for a quarter of a century, Niles settled in the isolated Black Hills community of Deadwood, South Dakota. There was no homecoming parade for Niles or any of the other five hundred thousand American troops who served their county in Vietnam. There were no crowds of well wishers to meet them at the airport, shake their hands, and thank them for their service. It was almost a stigma, a black mark, to have fought in Vietnam. The stories of ill treatment suffered by returning soldiers are legend—being pelted with eggs by antiwar protesters, or called "baby killers," or even shunned by close friends and family.

"We will never forget."

✳

Many returning Vietnam vets, bitter and burned out, just buried the memories and got on with their lives. Many have now gone decades without discussing the war with even their closest friends, not even those also in the military. The personal nightmares and flashbacks rarely ceased, but in public it was as if the Vietnam War—a war that lasted a dozen years and took the lives of fifty-five thousand Americans—had never happened.

But Niles Harris couldn't erase the memory of November 8. On that exact date every year for the next thirty-five years, he would get up, put on his old gray suit, go down to the local tavern, and lift a glass of whiskey in honor of all of his comrades who had died that day. This solemn ritual was his way of saying to old friends and their families, "We will never forget."

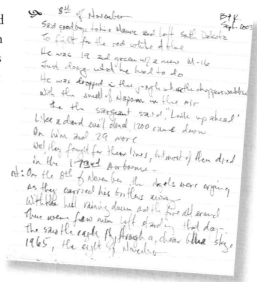

Kenny recorded the lyrics to "8th of November" in his journal in September 2003.

BIG AL'S

As we mentioned, our manager Marc Oswald had traveled out to Deadwood in the fall of 2004 and met a guy named Big Al, proud proprietor of one of Deadwood's finest drinking establishments, Big Al's Buffalo

Saloon and Bodega Bar. Somewhere in the conversation popped up the idea that we'd go out and play at Big Al's. Al's deal was simple: a plane ticket, room, board, and bar tab. Or as Niles Harris likes to say, "beans and sleep." We had a record deal by this point but no record. We were still coming up with songs.

So we pulled into Deadwood and performed at Big Al's. We more than made up for the lack of salary in free drinks. The bartender the first night was Niles Harris. As he served us drinks, Big Kenny complimented him on the beautiful handmade top hat he was wearing. It was created by an Indian artisan in the area named Michael McCloud. Hand-beaded and hand-stitched, it was a work of art.

The next day, Niles took us on a tour of some local gold mines, and he came up on the stage that night where we were playing and presented the hat to Big Kenny as a token of Deadwood hospitality. A beautiful friendship was born. Big Kenny now wears that hat proudly at almost every live performance of Big & Rich.

The "8th of November" video.

After we became closer, Niles told us his incredible Vietnam War story—the events of the November 8, 1965. Vietnam was not something either of us had experienced firsthand. Big Kenny was one year old when the war started; John wasn't even born. Our immediate response to Niles's story had nothing to do with politics. It had everything to do with men and women who put it all on the line. Neither of us has ever shot anybody or had a bullet shot at us. And there are hundreds of thousands of regular Americans out there who have that happen to them as a matter of duty.

Through Niles, we felt an instant connection to both his own terrible ordeal and the ordeal so many soldiers have gone through. So we figured we ought to write a song about it, since that's what we do for a living. As mentioned earlier, that trip to Deadwood inspired a number of Big

& Rich songs, from "Deadwood Mountain" to "Six Foot Town." But probably the most important song it inspired was our version of Niles's heroic tale—**"8th of November."**

MIKE LOVELACE

In November 2005, our second album, *Comin' to Your City,* was released on top of the single of the same name. That song was on the radio, climbing up the charts, and we were out doing shows in support of it. The new album also included **"8th of November,"** but that song had yet to be released as a single. In fact, we weren't even singing it in our live show. We had already produced the "8th of November" video, though, anticipating a later launch of the song.

"Greater love hath no man than to lay down his life for his brother."

✳

A brief word about that video, since it probably had as much to do with the success and reach of the song as the song itself. First of all, it was totally unlike anything we had ever tried to do. It not only had to tell, in a very concise and emotional way, the true story of a man who had fought in a war a long time ago, but also had to be almost a history lesson about that war. After all, to anyone under the age of thirty, Vietnam is something from the distant past. When someone that age thinks *war,* they think of either the first Gulf War, or 9/11, or the current war in Iraq. Vietnam is ancient history.

To help spell out that history, we began the video with our good friend Kris Kristofferson plainly telling the story of the 173rd Airborne and the events of 11/8/65, ending with the one message we hoped to convey with the song: "Greater love hath no man than to lay down his life for his brother."

Skillfully co-directed by Robert Deaton, George Flanigan, and Marc Oswald, the video mixes actual photos of the fallen soldiers from November 8 with archival footage of then-President Lyndon Johnson, jun-

BIG & RICH ON THE "8TH OF NOVEMBER" VIDEO

JOHN: "Pinnacle of our songwriting at this point. A pat on the back to Vietnam vets and what they had to go through . . ."

BIG KENNY: "A collection of a lot of people putting in a lot of effort. Very moving . . . a portrait of where a nineteen-year-old soldier was in 1965 and where he is today."

gle scenes of Vietnam, and the innocent young recruits of the 1960s, many of them draftees, getting their heads shaved as they headed off for war. Rather than this visual montage being a background to our song, our song almost becomes the soundtrack to this little movie, starring Niles Harris, about the nightmare of Vietnam. Which is exactly what we wanted—a lasting tribute to Niles, the 173rd, and American soldiers everywhere, at any time.

We carried this video with us when we went to Seattle to sing and promote *Comin' to Your City*. While we were there, a good friend of ours, radio station KMPS general manager Tony Thomas, told us that a lady had called the station to say her husband had served with Niles Harris in Vietnam and was there at the battle on November 8. Her name was Debbie Lovelace. We said, "Well, please, let's meet her."

Tony brought Debbie down to the show, and we all met up in John's bus. Obviously nervous, she told us her husband's experience of the battle and the aftermath, and we were, of course, touched by the story. Then we said, "Let us show you something," and put on a DVD of the video. Deeply moved, she asked if she could borrow the video to take back and show her husband.

"Sure," we said, "and better yet, we'd like to meet him." "He doesn't get out much," she said. "In fact, he hasn't been out of the house in four years." It turned out that her husband, Mike, had never recovered from the incredible stress of the war and never sought help for what was later diagnosed as PTSD, or post-traumatic stress disorder. He couldn't handle crowds. He hadn't ventured into a crowd of ten or more for decades.

A few months later, Tony Thomas shared this letter from Debbie with us:

"Guys, when you get to see the video I think that you, the vets that survived that day and the families of those that did not will be deeply touched. It is done with respect and honor and I must tell you that I cried through most of it because there were so many scenes that brought up the stories Mike has shared with me about that time. John told me that although they had originally thought it would be the first song/video released off the new CD they had recently changed their minds because he does not want this to just hit and fade . . . he wants to, as he put it, 'ramp up the release and make it as anticipated as it should be.' I can't begin to tell you how much it touched me seeing this labor of love and respect—John Rich is an amazing songwriter but he is an even more amazing man. It was quite obvious to me how much this project means to him.

"He also took the time to spend a few moments on the phone with Mike thanking him for his service and telling him that although he wished he could have been there and would have liked to meet him in person—he understood why he could not."

We later heard from Mike Lovelace that the song and video had encouraged him to go out and seek help. He had gone down to the local VA hospital and signed up for counseling. He was fighting his way back to normalcy after almost forty years of torment and grief.

We both choked up. We had never written a song that had changed someone's life so dramatically. And we knew that if Mike Lovelace felt that way about the song and the experience it recounted, then probably thousands of other Vietnam vets, and especially members of Niles's combat group, the 173rd Airborne, would feel the same.

About nine months after that first encounter with Mike's wife, we were back in Seattle, this time as part of Kenny Chesney's monster stadium tour. We played Quest Field Stadium before a crowd of fifty-two thousand people—the largest country show, someone said, in the history of Seattle. It was mammoth.

By this point, "8th of November" was a regular part of every show. When it came time to sing the song, complete with the Kris Kristofferson introduction on video, Big Kenny read aloud part of the letter Mike's wife had written us, then invited Mike on stage, along with Niles Harris and other proud vets. It was a turning point in Mike's life. A man who couldn't handle a crowd of ten a few months before was now holding the American flag and reciting the Pledge of Allegiance in front of fifty-two thousand. It was a remarkable transformation, and one man's unassailable testament to the power of music.

BELOW AND FOLLOWING PAGES: Performing "8th of November" at the Academy of Country Music Awards, 2006.

EXCERPTS FROM A LETTER TO NILES HARRIS

Dear Mr. Harris,

Thank you so much for sharing your story with Big & Rich. I can't begin to tell you how much it meant for my family to have the men of the 173rd Airborne honored and remembered . . . My name is Soren David Spickerman. My middle name is in honor of my Uncle David, 2nd Lieutenant David L. Ugland, killed in action in combat zone D on November 8th, 1965.

Even though David died before I was born, he has always been a big part of my life . . . I figured out at a young age how important he was to everybody in our family, especially my mother, Louise. She and David were real close, her being just a few years older than him. I remember Mom crying and being real sad every November 8th, and also on every birthday David would have had. I'll never forget one time when my Mom was especially down and weepy, when she explained to me that David had been dead longer than he'd been alive. She had actually figured it out to the exact day. On another occasion she was crying because she was having a hard time remembering what David's voice sounded like.

Every time I hear the song "8th of November" I have to suppress my emotion so that I don't start crying in front of people. The first time I heard the song I was by myself, and it hit me like a ton of bricks. I wept. That may sound a little odd since I never got to meet David, but our bond is a strong one nonetheless. I don't really know how to explain it. Only that I am extremely proud of him and what he stood for, the type of man he was. I feel like I knew him. I know that I love him . . .

Soren D. Spickerman
Neguanee, MI

**With General
Peter Pace and
Niles Harris in
Washington, DC.**

Mike, we had already come to realize, was only one of the many stories we came to hear about the 173rd Airborne, affectionately known as "The Herd," and the deep feelings that surviving members had for the friends they lost in Vietnam, feelings that they had cut themselves off from for years. As many of these vets have told us, in letter and in person, this one song opened the emotional floodgates for them. Either through direct contact or just bumping into a old friend at a concert, these men are getting back in touch after having virtually no communication for thirty-five or forty years. They're feeling a sense of community and comradeship again. They're feeling proud of what they went through and survived together.

At virtually every show we've done since the song was released as a single, veterans of the 173rd have shown up to see one another, recount old war stories, and reclaim an important part of their lives. Like all Vietnam vets, they needed to rid themselves of the bitter aftertaste of coming home from that war. This was finally an occasion for them to be thanked for their patriotic service.

From the moment "8th of November" hit, we realized that this song was going to eclipse and impact anything we had done previously. We saw it coming and prepared to get swept up in it. It hit Niles like a huge gust of wind blowing across the Dakota plains. One moment he's at home, quietly and privately commemorating his fellow soldiers every November 8. Next thing you know he's shaking hands with the chairman of the Joint Chiefs of Staff, General Peter Pace.

BACK TO VIETNAM

In September 2005, long before the record was released, we decided to produce a full-blown documentary centered on Niles returning to Vietnam after four decades to visit the battlefield and commemorate the lives of his comrades who had died that day. The brainstorm of the two of us and Marc Oswald, this again was something we'd never done—we

LEFT: The American and Vietnamese documentary film crews.

BELOW: While in Vietnam, we met with the man who was forced to give away the position of US troops, leading to the fatal battle on November 8, 1965.

ABOVE TOP AND ABOVE: Burying Niles's boots.

are in no way professional filmmakers—but something we thought we had to attempt.

At first, Niles had no interest in going back to that awful event in his young life. But he finally realized that it might be good for his friends, both living and dead, and a way to literally bury the past. Niles wanted to bury his Vietnam combat boots on that battlefield, as a tribute to his fallen brothers. So he signed on, and the four of us, along with a small documentary crew, took off for six unforgettable days in the Republic of Vietnam.

Skillfully written, directed, and produced by our friend Gary Chapman, the hour-long documentary follows us from Deadwood to—in Niles's words—"the same stinky, wet jungle" in Vietnam and the very spot where the battle took place. To the rest of our group, Vietnam was maybe the most exotic place we'd ever been, from Ho Chi Minh City to the Mekong Delta. The people were warm and friendly and apparently harbored no bitterness about the war in which millions of their countryman had died, including an untold number of civilians. To Niles, it was a return to sacred ground and perhaps a path to arriving at some kind of acceptance of what had happened there.

The boots that Niles had worn that day, still covered with the mud of the battlefield, had hung in his garage since he moved to Deadwood. It was time to return them to their rightful resting place. In a brief ceremony, Niles dug a hole and buried those boots on the battlefield. We all took a shot of whiskey, like Niles had done every eighth day of November for forty long years, and we sang our little ballad as an end note. Then we headed back home.

The song **"8th of November"** has become a permanent part of the identity of Big & Rich. The video reached award status; the documentary aired on GAC TV and has been distributed in more than a million DVDs. But the saga of November 8 and the 173rd Airborne Brigade didn't end there. There was a lot more to come.

BELOW LEFT: Big Kenny on the Mekong River.

BELOW: John meets a young woman on her way to school.

KATIE DARNELL

Long before we met Niles Harris at the Buffalo Saloon and Bodega Bar—in fact, long before we were the duo Big & Rich—we came together to promote something larger than ourselves. It involved a sixteen-year-old girl named Katie Darnell. It was Christmastime 2000, and we had separately been asked to visit the Vanderbilt Children's Hospital in Nashville and sing a few songs to some very sick kids. That's where we met Katie, struggling to survive her third bout of brain cancer and many torturous rounds of radiation and chemotherapy. As the two of us and guitarist Adam Shoenfeld got ready to perform a couple of tunes for her, Katie abruptly announced that she had a song she had written while sitting in church one day, and she wanted to sing it to *us*. We said, No problem, you go first.

Katie sat up, sipped a little water, and proceeded to belt out her own composition, called "Rescue Me." As Big Kenny later described the experience, it was like being hit right in the chest with a sixteen-pound sledgehammer.

"What do you do when you're scared inside?
When all of your feelings just seem to collide . . .
I love thee, rescue me, shine your light, lead me home
Lord, all I need is your love, rescue me . . ."

The song hit us so strongly that we decided to go into a studio where, with a little help from our friends, we made the first recording of "Rescue Me." We then grabbed a boom box and played the song back to Katie in the hospital. She approved. Soon it found its way into the hands of Gerry House of WSIX in Nashville, who played it on the air. The phones went nuts. Katie Darnell's "Rescue Me" was a hit!

That song, and the power of Katie's example, took her to a lot of places. First off, it took her to her high school prom with the two of us as her dates. She also ended up being invited to Walt Disney World in Orlando, to the stage of the Grand Ole Opry, and foremost, to Washington, DC. Having been designated Vanderbilt Children's Hospital am-

LEFT: John Rich and Katie Darnell.

BELOW: Katie Darnell's high school prom photo.

"A Night Beneath The Stars"
CCHS Jr-Sr Prom
May 4, 2002
Studio III

bassador, Katie attended an event in 2001 called the Children's Miracle Network "Champions Across America," and with John at her side performed her song for President George W. Bush and First Lady Laura Bush. In Katie's words, "It was so cool!"

Along the way, we wrote a song about Katie called **"She's a Butterfly,"** and the lovely and talented Martina McBride recorded it for one of her albums. Martina got to know Katie and even called her only a few days before she died. There is no classier woman in country music than Martina McBride.

Katie Darnell passed away in 2004, but her song lives on. "Rescue Me" was nominated for a Dove Award and has been recorded by the two of us and Wynonna. It's never been released in a Big & Rich version, but it certainly will someday.

One trip to the hospital, one sick little girl, one song—it not only changed her shortened life forever, it changed ours, too.

ABOVE: Performing "Rescue Me" at the Grand Ole Opry.

RIGHT: With Katie Darnell's family in 2005.

ALONG THE WAY

Like many of the Mafia members, Katie Darnell
adopted John's grandmother as her Granny Rich. She wrote
this poem for her, which now hangs in a treasured place in
Granny Rich's tailoring shop.

ALONG THE WAY

Along life's great path, God put you,
Another person whose love is strong and True.
Someone to think of me and care
For me along the way.
A love and a prayer I can depend on each day.
A friend like you is hard to find.
Yes, I'm proud and thankful to have you as
A good friend of mine.
God gives us many blessing through
The bad times,
And many times we wonder why,
But just wait and He just might reveal the
Answer right before your eyes.
John, Lisa and Big Kenny were the blessings
Behind the first door,
And it led to another door that had even
More!

LOVE,
KATIE
2001

DARFUR

Since we became Big & Rich, it's been a huge part of our musical agenda to gravitate to those points of light like Niles and Katie and try to effect the world in some small way. It is part of what John calls our "evangelistic DNA"—we just like to tell people about things that could use their attention and maybe even their active help. When you look around, you can get swept up into some pretty awesome tragedies. Perhaps the largest such area of public concern we've ever been a part of is the worldwide campaign to stop the genocide going on in the southern part of Sudan called Darfur.

What, you might ask, are two country boys doing getting involved in a problem taking place halfway around the world in an area they've never been and effecting people they know almost nothing about? It didn't take much. Maybe it began with Big Kenny's great-aunt giving his family a subscription to *National Geographic* every Christmas, instilling in Big Kenny a fascination with the global community. Technically, it began when the wife of our record guru, Paul Worley, invited Big Kenny to hear a speaker appearing before a group called Tennesseans Against Genocide. Politics aside, Darfur is a clear-cut horror of historic magnitude—a population of people is in the process of being wiped out.

The extent of the genocide in Darfur is hard to comprehend. The

Arab-controlled government of Sudan, largely through the use of nongovernmental mercenaries, is slaughtering hundreds of thousands of African Sudanese in a campaign of massive ethnic cleansing. A reported four hundred thousand or more people have died, and millions have been displaced and are barely surviving in refugee camps. There are official efforts to stop this slaughter, but the killing goes on. Remote southwestern Sudan, unfortunately, does not have large oil reserves or diamond mines or any other valuable resources that the world pays attention to. It just has people being tortured, raped, and killed.

Meeting with George Clooney at the Save Darfur rally in Washington, DC.

It may seem foolish to some that we spend our time involved in this African issue, but once we found out what was going on, it never crossed our minds *not* to try to help in some way. In the same way that Spike Lee applies his talents to a four-hour documentary on the Katrina disaster, or Bono spends much of his life creating his "One" project and lobbying heads of state to focus on the myriad problems in Africa, we just want to participate in the world and hopefully foment a little positive change.

To share a stage with former Secretary of State Madeline Albright and other world leaders as we did in massive "Save Darfur" rallies in New York and Washington in 2006 was not a duty. It was a privilege. It gives us a sense of connection with the whole world. It's also why we hang a SAVE DARFUR banner on stage at every one of our shows. If just a handful of people in the audience go home and Google "Darfur" on their computer, we will add a few more voices to the rising worldwide chorus to end the hateful killing of innocent people in northern Africa.

What more can we do? We think about that every day. Big Kenny is currently playing with the idea of flying a hundred thousand people into Chad, the country next to Sudan, and have them march hand in hand across the border and into the refugee camps of all of those suffering, displaced people. Sound crazy? Remember "We Are the World"? "Live Aid"? "Hands Across America"? As soon as we've figured out the details, we'll let you know.

A DAY OF HONOR

The song **"8th of November"** quickly fed into a national campaign to honor all the men and women who have served, or are currently serving, in the 173rd Airborne Brigade. That campaign centered in the construction of a memorial at Fort Benning, Georgia, much like the Vietnam Memorial in Washington that honors all fifty-five thousand Americans who gave their lives in Vietnam. This campaign led to one of our greatest nights on stage—October 7, 2006.

The effort to build a lasting memorial at Fort Benning, where the original 173rd Airborne paratroopers were trained, started long before we got involved with the unit. We just came along to hopefully speed things up a little. We figured a big fund-raising concert—called "A Day of Honor"—would be the best way to help.

The location was the HiFi Buys Amphitheatre in Atlanta, and all proceeds would go to the memorial. No one was getting paid for this gig. As it so happened, Lynyrd Skynyrd—recent Rock and Roll Hall of Fame inductees—were headlining the night before our concert, and the minute we told them what we were up to, we combined forces. We also had Cowboy Troy, the great John Anderson, and the Lost Trailers to add to the festivities. The call went out and the Mafia Soldiers/Freak Paraders arrived, sixteen thousand strong. They were joined by dozens of both surviving 173rd veterans and Gold Star Mothers from all over the country.

Many of these veterans just hopped on a plane and came to this re-

union unannounced. As one "sky soldier," Terry Napier from Kennett, Missouri, told a bystander, "I don't know these guys, Big & Rich—in fact, when I bought their album a couple of months back, it was the first country album I had ever bought. But if they were standing here right now, I'd tell them that what they have done for the 173rd has really touched my heart. Really touched my heart. It's given a new meaning to my life."

The concert in Atlanta was an all-day event. The goal was to raise half a million dollars to put the memorial fund over the line. Special VIP seats down front sold for a thousand bucks a pop—and they were full.

"THE MOST IMPORTANT THING IN MY LIFE"

We received this heartfelt letter from Deb Yashinski from Richlands, North Carolina, a participant in the Atlanta concert and a proud Gold Star Mother of Sergeant Michael Yashinski, a member of the 173rd Airborne who was killed in Kirkuk, Iraq, on December 24, 2003.

"...Words can not truly express how we felt about being there in Atlanta. You made us feel so welcomed and loved. Being treated like a queen has truly been a balm to my soul. You see, that was how Michael always treated me. Also, because all of you got to know me and the rest of the 173rd vets, I hope that you got an insight into who Michael was and because of that, he will always be remembered. And that is the most important thing in my life."

Of course you could sit on the grass for fifteen dollars and have just as good a time.

The day began with a morning 120-mile motorcycle ride through central Georgia into the amphitheater. At a press conference later in the afternoon, we were welcomed by the governor of Georgia, Sonny Perdue, and honored by the endorsement of some high-ranking army brass. Niles was blown away.

"This is something else. I mean, from that little meeting in Deadwood to here is just amazing. There's enough brass back here for a general court-martial. And it would have been a shaky thing thirty years ago. But this is something else."

Perhaps no one put things in perspective better than one of the attending brass, former 173rd commander Brigadier General James Yarborough:

"I think it really does talk a lot about what our country is today. You've got a great brigade, on point for the country of Vietnam for seven years. The first combat unit developed to Vietnam, the last combat unit to come home in 1972. One thousand four hundred and seventy killed in action, names on the Vietnam Veterans' Memorial up in Washington, DC . . ."

"This event is not only a tribute to a great brigade, to the original sky soldiers and the sky soldiers serving today, but also a tribute to the thousands of men and women across America—they're not just soldiers, they're sailors, airmen, and marines. It's a tribute to them, too. Across the world . . ."

The surprise of the press conference came when one of our partners in the event, our dear friend Victor Sansone, the president and general manager of Atlanta radio stations WKHX and WYAY, announced the total amount of gate receipts and pledges, all going to the memorial fund: almost six hundred thousand dollars. This announcement was a very gratifying moment for everyone involved.

Marc Oswald and Big Kenny and Christiev lead the motorcycle ride to Atlanta (John followed in his Corvette).

And it was a hell of a concert! Looking out at a sea of handheld American flags and a front row full of decorated veterans, we played our hearts out. When it came time to play "8th of November," out marched an honor corps with the flag that include Niles Harris, fellow vets Don Dali, Sonny Barto, Joe Queen, Craig Ford, Tom Marrinan, Don Bliss, and Thomas Keene, and Gold Star Mothers Deb Yashinski, Alma Hart, Gail Berstein, and Gail

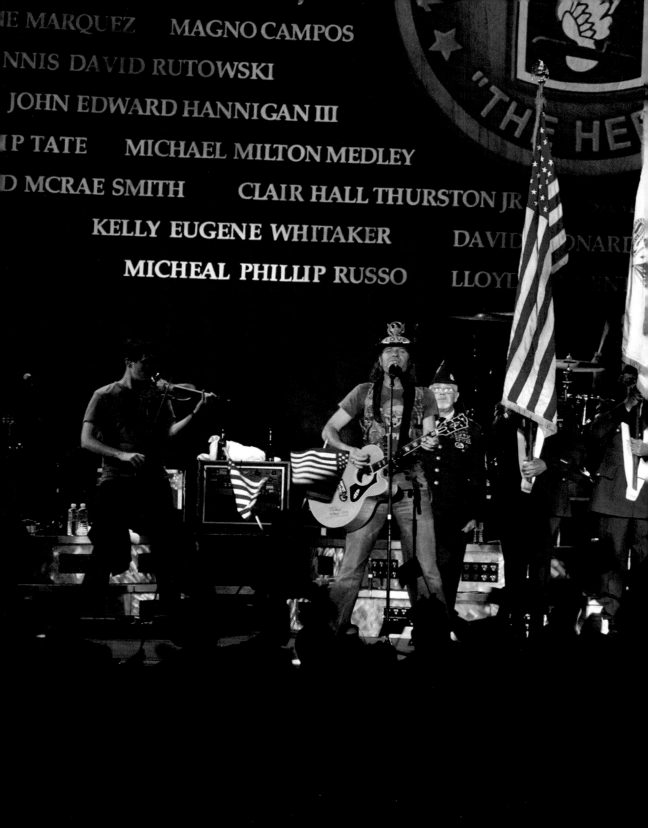

JOHN ALBERT HUGHLETT

DAVID LATTIMORE KEEL   DAVIS UPTAIN

RICHARD LEE NUZIARD   JAMES BELTON

CHARLES LEROY MITCHELL JR

WAYNE WARREN HUMPHRIES

STANLEY TOLLIVER   THOMAS ALFRED TURNAGE

GLAND   SAMUEL ARLEN EIDSON

EENE   AMES ARTHUR NATHAN

Performing "8th of November" in Atlanta on October 6, 2006,
with Vietnam veterans of the 173rd Airborne Brigade.

The model of the 173rd Memorial to be built at Fort Benning, Georgia, and some of the many people who helped make it happen (from left to right): Colonel (Retired) Ken Smith (former President of the 173rd Airborne Brigade Association); Victor Sansone, manager of WKHX-FM, KICKS, and WYAY—The Eagle, Atlanta; Gold Star Mother Mrs. Alma Hart (mother of PFC John Hart killed in Iraq in 2004); Niles Harris; Cowboy Troy; Lynyrd Skynyrd's lead singer Johnny Van Zant; Lynyrd Skynyrd's lead guitarist Rickey Medlocke; Al Rascon, Medal of Honor recipient from 1967 battle; Big Kenny; John Rich; Terry Modglin, President, 173rd Airborne Brigade National Memorial Foundation; Brigadier General James Yarbrough.

Michaels. We had presented the flag and led the audience in the Pledge of Allegiance dozens of times before this night, but nothing prepared us for the response we felt from that crowd in Atlanta. As one general said at the press conference, this tribute was a way of bringing closure to many men who had suffered in silence for decades. It was also a way for the rest of us to finally pay our respects for their service.

To cap things off, Colonel (Retired) Kenneth Smith stepped forward and handed awards to the two of us: special commendations from the secretary of the army that officially made us members of the 173rd Airborne Brigade. We've earned our share of awards in country music, but none even comes close to this one.

We both look forward to the day we stand next to Niles and his band of brothers in Fort Benning, Georgia, and witness the unveiling of the permanent memorial for the 173rd Airborne Brigade. The recognition that the song and video of "8th of November" has received will fade in time, but that memorial will be there forever. And for us, anyway, it all started in a bar in Deadwood, South Dakota, with an unforgettable war story from a pretty decent bartender.

Niles Harris in His Own Words

✻

Q: How did you end up in Deadwood?

NILES: I ran out of gas.

Q: Where did you grow up?

NILES: I haven't grown up yet.

Q: You really ran out of gas?

NILES: Nah, I just liked the way Deadwood looked. The Black Hills are great and I enjoy the area and so that's where I ended up. Bought a neat old 1882 house and I can sit in my yard and watch deer.

Q: How big is Deadwood?

NILES: In the winter, about fifteen hundred, in the summer, maybe eighteen hundred. It's a tourist town, like Virginia City, Nevada.

Q: Did it surprise you when Big & Rich said they were going to write a song about November 8?

NILES: Hell, yeah. Over a year's time, they would call every once in a while and ask about this thing or that. Then it all just started happening. It's crazy.

Q: How did the word get out about the memorial, besides Big & Rich?

NILES: A paratrooper's a paratrooper, just like a marine's a marine. The word just spread.

Q: Did you ever ask Big & Rich why they took such an interest in your story?

NILES: Nah, I didn't have to. These guys are the real deal. I didn't have to ask them anything. Whether these guys were Vietnam vets or not never entered my mind or theirs. It was just the right thing to do.

Standing with Niles Harris in front of a truck decorated to honor the 173rd Airborne Brigade members.

NO PLACE LIKE HOME

JOHN: "I get a lot of pleasure out of work. Hey, if what you do for a living is giving you a bigger buzz than taking a vacation from it, why would you take a vacation?"

BIG KENNY: "Lincoln's a year old, and he already grooves, you know, plays the drums with two sticks, one in each hand ... he's already got music all around ... he's my soul, man."

A HUGE BUZZ

As you've probably gathered by now, we spend a lot of time on the road in one capacity or another. As many an artist will tell you, the road is a double-edged sword. It can be a highway of adventure and excitement, or a highway of loneliness and rootlessness. The best antidote to not getting strung out on the road is to have something waiting for you when you get back home.

Big Kenny has a wife and a new baby. John has a million friends, Granny Rich and the rest of his clan, and musical projects away from Big & Rich that provide him a bigger buzz than any vacation he could think of.

Christiev, Big Kenny, and Lincoln on vacation. John and Frank kick back at home.

ABOVE TOP: John and Gretchen.

ABOVE: John's Corvette.

With the success of Big & Rich, both of us have been afforded some great opportunities to expand our musical horizons. We both like to write material on our own and work with other artists. At this juncture in his life, this is especially true for John. John was a successful songwriter in Nashville before Big & Rich, and the songs he and Big Kenny have written together have only enhanced that reputation. When the world got wind of songs that John had co-written like **"Save a Horse (Ride a Cowboy),"** among many B&R hits, and "Redneck Woman"—the overnight number one single he wrote with Gretchen Wilson—artists and producers in Nashville started rifling through his song catalog, looking for another hit. Since his catalog of original songs written and demoed was somewhere over a thousand strong at that point, there was a lot of new music to pick over.

It created a snowball effect. Everyone in town wanted a John Rich

JOHN RICH'S SONGS

These are just a few of the songs John has written or co-written (several with Big Kenny) that have recently been released by other artists.

"All Jacked Up"—Gretchen Wilson
"Amarillo Sky"—Jason Aldean
"Attitude"—Wynonna
"Come to Bed"—Gretchen Wilson
"Hicktown"—Jason Aldean
"Like We Never Loved at All"—Faith Hill and Tim McGraw
"Mississippi Girl"—Faith Hill
"Pickin' Wildflowers"—Keith Anderson
"Redneck Woman"—Gretchen Wilson
"She's a Butterfly"—Martina McBride
"Sunshine & Summertime"—Faith Hill
"A Woman Knows"—John Anderson
"Why"—Jason Aldean

song for their next album. Since March 2004, about the time when both "Save a Horse" and "Redneck Woman" came out, John has had just short of two hundred original songs recorded and released. There are songs out there now that John wrote more than ten years ago. No one wanted them then. Now everyone wants them. So go fate and fortune in Nashville.

John's songwriting prowess is legendary in Music City. For the last two years, he has been honored as the ASCAP Songwriter of the Year. (ASCAP is one of three major performing rights organization in the music business.) John-penned songs mentioned in his 2006 ASCAP award presentation include our own song **"Big Time,"** along with Gretchen Wilson's "All Jacked Up," the Faith Hill song "Mississippi Girl," and Keith Anderson's "Pickin' Wildflowers."

John's acceptance speech at the big ASCAP ceremony at the Ryman

Auditorium in Nashville, the holy shrine of country music, pretty much summed up the depth of his gratitude. **"I'm a pretty cocky dude. I bring my liquor to the party, but tonight, I am humbled. I'm in awe. I don't necessarily deserve this, but I'll take it."**

You'd think that being named the best songwriter in Nashville, if not the whole damn country, would be enough, but not for John—not for either of us, really. John doesn't just write songs with and for other artists in his Big & Rich downtime. He goes into the studio and produces albums for a whole array of artists, from Gretchen Wilson to Cowboy Troy to John Anderson. He just finished an album with Muzik Mafia Mafioso James Otto, and is developing a live album and DVD with the Muzik Mafia co-founder and Godfather Jon Nicholson.

John travels in style.

As we are writing this book, John is in the process of producing anywhere from four to six albums a year. Last year he spent more than a hundred days in a studio on top of everything we did in Big & Rich. You've heard of gym rats? John, at this point in his career, is a bit of a studio rat. His life is submerged in music and the business of music.

When John's not in the studio, he's probably out and about in Nashville, tearing up the town with his friends. Studio work aside, it's hard to come off the road singing to ten thousand people a night, at 120 decibels, for two weeks at a time and then just sit around the house. When nine o'clock comes around, the time you usually hit the stage, you get a little antsy crashed in front of the TV with a take-out pizza, watching *20/20*. Unless you're exhausted, you go out.

So John and his cronies hit the bars. This is not only fun, but also educational. In a multicultural place like Nashville, especially for college-aged kids and those in their twenties and early thirties, even a country bar is no longer monolithically country. Half of the music you hear in a lot of such bars is urban or pop music.

There's a bar in Nashville that John likes to frequent called Silverado's, an eighteen-and-up establishment. Drop by sometime. For every country song you hear, like something by George Strait, you'll hear an urban rap/dance tune by Ludacris. Or you'll hear "Big City" by Merle Haggard followed by "Gold Digger" by Kanye West. To these kids, the old musical demarcations just don't apply anymore.

Why? Because to them, it's just music. If they want to hear something sad and country, on comes George Jones. If they want to shake their tail feather, George won't do. You need Nelly and his ilk. It's just what fits the mood.

John is out there checking it out. He's liable to show up at a fraternity party at Vanderbilt, places someone like John wouldn't normally frequent, just to hear what those frat boys are jamming to. Sometimes he's recognized, sometimes he's not. Most of the time he's just having a good time, soaking up the music and the culture. It all gets filed away somewhere in his brain, and the next time we get together to write a song, some mixture of musical ideas inspired by that frat affair is liable to come out. It is part of the ongoing experiment called Big & Rich.

And the same goes for producing albums for other artists. He gets a huge buzz and enormous satisfaction out of the interaction between his own musical skills and instincts and someone coming from a totally different place. John is in no way a hip-hop artist, or even a *hick*-hop artist,

JOHN'S TRUCK

Jimmy Buster was my best friend. He had been my soundman through the Lonestar years and through my solo career. He had five kidney transplants in his life, and

before his last one, he gave me power of attorney in case he ended up on life support at some point. Three months later, he got a staph infection that took over his entire body. He ended up on life support at Vanderbilt, and I was faced with having to sign the papers to take him off the support. Thank God he passed just hours before I had to make that decision. At his funeral, which my dad preached at and I sang at, I talked to his mother about this old truck, a '64 Ford F150 shortbed, that Buster had been telling me about. She said it was in a barn in the country, and I asked permission to purchase it. I bought the truck and had it completely restored to show truck condition. There is a plaque in the cab that says, "My brother Jimmy Buster, always ridin' with you." This poem by Jimmy is proudly displayed in my house.

If I should ever leave this world
Try to Remember all the good times.
Days filled with sunshine and laughter
With just a little bit of Rain.

And if you should look back
Forget all the bad times,
The lonely, sad and blue times,
But never forget the Rain.

For the Rain is God's way of
Cleansing the earth, to keep
     nature pure.
Like Tears are God's way of
Releasing sadness and
Cleansing the mind.

Someone said: Always remember me
In laughter if only in tears
Than not at all.

I disagree, I hope everyone
Remembers me with joyous tears
From laughter
From the thoughts of ME.

JIMMY BUSTER

Jimmy and John.

ABOVE: Brian McKnight helps John Rich celebrate his birthday.

LEFT: John at his birthday bash with Cowboy Troy and his wife, Laura.

but working alongside Cowboy Troy allows him to step into that world and love it. The same with working with someone like Gretchen Wilson or Faith Hill. He doesn't have to be a Mississippi girl or a redneck woman to connect with that view of the world. To help someone like Gretchen get her heart and soul on tape, John has to get into her mind, and understand her angle on life, for months at a time. Inevitably, he walks away a richer man and a richer songwriter.

Okay, John doesn't work all the time. Some days he wiles away the time playing with his trusty, 150-pound American bulldog, Frank Sinatra Rich. Every Sunday that he's in town, he and Frank try to make it out to Granny Rich's place, have Sunday dinner with his relatives, including his dad, and just relax. That's his big stabilizer: talking about football or World War II with his grandfather Pap Rich, or religion with his father, or any subject, really, other than the business of country music.

Right now, though, the work drives him. Vacations to the South Seas or even a getaway in the Grand Tetons can wait. Ten years from now (or maybe sooner) he could be like Big Kenny, still working hard but also spending every day and night possible with the wife and kids.

PAP RICH

"If it weren't for guns and American people that knew how to use them, everyone in this country would either be saluting a swastika or living under the flag of the rising sun."

That was a phrase that I heard all of my life. The man who lived by these words, a member of The Greatest Generation, was my grandfather, William Melvin Rich, or as the family called him, "Pap." On average, over 1,000 World War II veterans die every day in this country. My own personal WWII hero passed away before the completion of this book on December 14, 2006, one day after his eightieth birthday. From the ages of eighteen to twenty-one, he was a member of the very first Special Forces group in the United States Army. Before the Seals, before the Rangers, before Delta Force, there were these few men. They were known as the OSSF—"Office of Strategic Service Forces."

After World War II, the OSSF was disbanded, and became the precursor group to our modern day CIA. A recent film, *The Good Shepherd,* depicts the brave men of the OSSF. They were highly trained and highly motivated to defeat the Japanese in the Pacific Theater. They were sent on the most dangerous and most covert operations of any unit in the entire armed forces at that time.

During his tenure with the OSSF, Pap Rich sustained injuries that garnered him six Purple Hearts, the Bronze Star, and many other awards. He used to joke, "The only two accommodations I never received were the Medal of Honor, and the Good Conduct award!" His weapons of choice were the Thompson submachine gun and the flamethrower, and his job description was "tunnel rat." His daily mission was to go into an opening of a cave and flush the enemy out the other side. It was deadly work; my grandfather had over 500 confirmed kills during his time in WWII.

At numerous times, he had to undergo detoxification for dependency on morphine, due to all of his painful war injuries. He had been burned, shot in the gut, bayoneted in the back, butted in the head by a rifle stock, and hit with a white phosphorus grenade. Many immediate family members and good friends never made it back from that war, and most mornings I would have a cup of coffee with him and watch him tear up talking about those men, and how he should have never made it back.

A few days before he died, I was with him in the hospital with my little brother Isaac, and my Pap said something that in a million years would have never entered my mind. He said, "You know, dropping the big bombs on Japan

BELOW: John wears Pap Rich's World War II uniform.

William Melvin
Rich.

made us soldiers so damn mad!" I said,
"Mad, why?" He said, "It made us mad
because it ended the war. We wanted to
invade mainland Japan and kill every
single one of those sons of bitches."

I said, "Well Pap, think of how many American lives
we would have lost, maybe even your own life." He said,
"Trust me, it would have been worth it!"

He was without a doubt the absolute toughest, most
dedicated, non-bending, fiercest patriot I've ever known. He
was a real Rambo, a genuine American hero. He had a major
impact on my way of thinking of how I go about my life. He
used to tell me, "John, the fight's not over till the other man
can't get up." I've taken that attitude toward anything that
gets in the way of spreading "music without prejudice."

There are a lot of obstacles in the world that have tried
to impede the forward progress of the idea of "freedom of
musical expression." From Big & Rich music, to Cowboy
Troy, to the whole general principles of the Muzik Mafia,
me and my partners in music have fought like hell for our
right to create art without boundaries.

If I were a soldier, I'd hope to be like my grandfather,
but I'm not. I'm a musician. But the lessons I learned from
that man, and the DNA that he passed on to me, will stay
with me forever, whether it be in music or somewhere as
distant as the White House. Some people consider me a
hard ass, and I probably am. I understand when Kenny says,
"Love Everybody." It's a good thing to try to do; however,
there are wolves in the world that want to eat the flock. It
takes a lion to kill a wolf. My grandfather was a lion.

To quote retired Sgt. William Melvin Rich, United Stated
Army:

"If you don't love America, why don't you just get the hell
outta here right now!"

Indeed, sir, indeed.

John Rich

FAMILY MAN

Big Kenny was a full-time carouser and troublemaker until he ran into a certain woman during the production of Gretchen Wilson's "Redneck Woman" video. Her name was Christiev, and she was the wardrobe stylist on the shoot. Christiev had grown up in New York and Las Vegas, the daughter of Chico Holiday, a veteran nightclub entertainer now turned minister and Christian singer. Her mother was a world-champion baton twirler and worked for years at the Playboy Club in New York. Christiev had been around show business most of her life and had learned one important rule: Never date an artist. As her mother once told her: "If you ever meet a man with a guitar, turn around and run."

Big Kenny and Christiev with her sons, Christopher and Cameron, and their son, Lincoln.

"If you ever meet a man with a guitar, turn around and run."

As Christiev tells the story, she was totally exhausted from working on the video shoot, and in walked this guy in a top hat and smoking jacket. She gave him a quick once-over then blurted out, "So, who are you?" Big Kenny turned around and announced, *"I'm Big Kenny."* Christiev had never heard of him and never heard any Big & Rich music. They immediately got into a conversation about his real name; Christiev only found out by asking him what was on his birth certificate. It was pretty much downhill after that.

A couple of days later, Big Kenny was asking for her phone number. Christiev hesitated—this guy was clearly an artist. But Big Kenny won her over quickly. He said, *"Hey, I just wanted to know if you want another friend."* As Christiev remembers, she was at a time in her life when that was a really sweet sentence to her heart.

There was one more barrier Christiev had to get over. At the time, she wasn't a huge country fan. Though she lived and worked in Nashville, her taste in country music leaned toward the outer fringes of Lyle Lovett or Bonnie Raitt. What if she didn't like Big Kenny's music? "Lord," she recalls praying silently, "please, please, let me love it." And, of course, she did.

But they couldn't work together—another of Christiev's hard-and-fast rules about boyfriends. They kept their dating close to the vest while Big Kenny and John went out to promote **"Save a Horse (Ride a Cowboy)"** and Christiev's friends started chiding her for breaking the don't-date-artists rule. Finally, Big Kenny called one day and asked her to revisit her "mission statement" regarding working together. Big Kenny was not just another artist; he was also, she soon realized, more than just a big party guy. He was, in her words, "a deep-hearted soul who really tried to live up to his motto of 'Love Everybody.' "

Having revised pretty much all of her mission statements about men, Christiev next worked on the "Save a Horse (Ride a Cowboy)" video and came to understand what made both of us tick. It's from a lyric Big Kenny was working on at the time: **"Big hat, no cattle ain't the way I work."** In other words, she now says, "They both were intent on staying true to who they were," no matter what others thought. As a stylist, she could see this right away. If John wanted to wear a green jacket or a lot of jewelry or rhinestone-studded blue jeans, he did. If Big Kenny wanted to wear an undershirt and a long captain's jacket from the turn of the century, well, there you go. What you see is what you get.

Once the courtship was out of the box, Big Kenny and Christiev moved pretty fast. All the craziness around the first single and first album broke over that first summer they were together, but they were rarely apart for very long. Big Kenny was on top of the world and was just

Marc Oswald, Big Kenny, Christiev, Kristin Barlowe, Mista D, and Greg Oswald on the way to the wedding.

being discovered by the unattached women of America, but Christiev wasn't too worried. Big Kenny had been around for a while. He wasn't going to blow a good thing.

So one day, about nine or ten months after they had met, Big Kenny turned to Christiev and said, **"Well, I was hoping we could find a weekend to get married."** Christiev's reply: "Well, all right, let's do that." They decided this on a Monday, and by that Friday they were on a private plane with four of their dearest friends, heading toward Deadwood, South Dakota.

Another reason Big Kenny wanted to get married around that time was that he wanted the wedding close to Valentine's Day so it would be easy to remember their anniversary. Christiev had a better idea. What about January 23, or "1–2–3." Could he remember that? That was the date, for sure.

The next morning, Big Kenny got up to write a little poem that was later used as the press release about the marriage. He then went out to scout a suitable location for the wedding. He came back and announced, **"I know where we're going to get married. On Tatonka. Where Kevin Costner shot his epic Academy Award–winning film _Dances with Wolves_. At high noon."**

Mista D, aka Damien Horne, an ordained minister, had come along to perform the ceremony. The wedding party got to the spot, Tatonka, and it was closed for the day. So the whole party, including Christiev in her wedding outfit, hopped the fence. Big Kenny and Christiev went to the top of a hill by themselves to look out over a vista of hundreds of miles of South Dakota wilderness. They rode up on a borrowed classic Harley motorcycle. Then Big Kenny plopped down on one knee, showed her the ring, and asked her, **"Will you marry me and spend the rest of your life with me and be the mother of my children?"**

When she said yes, Christiev remembers, Big Kenny yelled down to the wedding party at the bottom of the hill, "She said yes! Please get up here before she changes her mind!"

BIG KENNY'S POEM TO CHRISTIEV

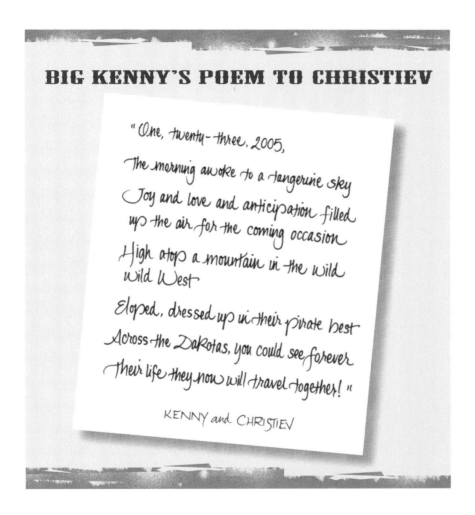

"One, twenty-three, 2005,
The morning awoke to a tangerine sky
Joy and love and anticipation filled
up the air, for the coming occasion
High atop a mountain in the wild
wild West

Eloped, dressed up in their pirate best
Across the Dakotas, you could see forever
Their life they now will travel together!"

KENNY and CHRISTIEV

"She said yes! Please get up here before she changes her mind!"

✳

And there they were married, Big Kenny dressed like a cleaned-up pirate in his top hat and finest vested jacket, and Christiev in what Big Kenny described as a pirate-maiden outfit. As Christiev later noted, "It was the perfect location. We could see forever."

LEFT: Big Kenny and Christiev tie the knot.

ABOVE: "You may now kiss the bride."

LINCOLN WILLIAM HOLIDAY ALPHIN

The very night of their wedding, Big Kenny and Christiev decided they wanted to have kids right away. They wasted no time. Within a month Christiev was pregnant. Big Kenny was on the road when Christiev found out, and since she didn't want to tell him on the phone, she waited until he got home to break the news. Big Kenny went nuts.

"My swimmers work!" he shouted. My swimmers really, really work!"

Through most of her pregnancy, Christiev traveled with Big Kenny. They were just married and, as Christiev puts it, "We don't do well apart." Big Kenny told Christiev that he needed her out on the road for "protection"—protection from the hoards of adoring lasses waiting to meet him nightly.

The initial due date was exactly Big Kenny's birthday, November 1. Since the birth was going to be via C-section, they moved the date to November 2, so the baby didn't have to compete with the old man for presents. They found out it was a boy only after Christiev had given

BELOW: Baby Lincoln meets the world.

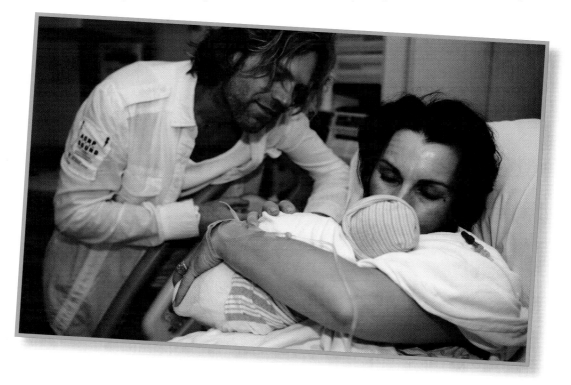

birth. The name they arrived at combined three distinct elements. *Lincoln,* after Big Kenny's all-time favorite American statesman, Abraham Lincoln. *William,* which is Big Kenny's father's name and his own first name. And *Holiday,* in tribute to Christiev's father's stage name, Chico Holiday. Lincoln William Holiday Alphin. Or as both parents might say, Lincoln William "Every day is a Holiday" Alphin. John Rich has the honor of being Lincoln's Godfather.

Christiev's new role soon became both Lincoln's mother and road manager. With Big Kenny on the road constantly, the job was to get him and his son together as much as possible. By the time he was four weeks old, Lincoln and Mom were on Big Kenny's touring bus. Big Kenny would do a show, then get up in the middle of the night to take care of the boy while Christiev continued to recover from surgery. It's a big job being Big Kenny and Big Dad Kenny at the same time.

Back home, Lincoln hangs with Big Kenny wherever he is. Big Kenny props him up so that he can watch him write and play around on the piano and guitar. Lincoln has been awash in music since the day he was born. Christiev takes him out to every show she can and even outfits him with his own little set of headphones. When he sees those headphones, he knows exactly what's coming. To complete the picture, Christiev ordered a pint-size top hat for Lincoln from the man who makes Big Kenny's elaborate hats. At under a year old, it'll take him awhile to grow into it.

Christiev has Lincoln ready to see Daddy perform.

Big Kenny at home, according to Christiev, is much quieter and more serious than Big Kenny on stage. In her words, "He's like an Australian sheepdog. He's got to have a job to do."

Puppy Frank gives
baby Lincoln a kiss.

Big Kenny, Christiev and Lincoln take a winter vacation.

Big Kenny always has side projects, both musical and nonmusical. When he's not on the computer digging up information about the situation in Darfur, he's trying to figure out how to install solar energy panels in the home he owns in Virginia. Or he's cooking. Or he's showing Lincoln how to play the drums. Or he's plotting another family adventure to some distant part of the world.

Christiev has the perfect term to describe both of us in our time away from our work life of Big & Rich. We both, she says, have an advanced case of ADS. Always Doing Something Syndrome.

MILK AND BEER

While John is off writing songs for other artists and producing albums for people like Cowboy Troy and John Anderson, Big Kenny is doing the same. He's working on albums with artists like Mista D and currently

WE'RE THE PIRATES OF COOKIETOWN!

"And we are the Pirates of Cookie Town
Bohemian Vikings we live off our likings
And laugh till the sun goes down
We're brothers of bravery and robbers
* of love*
We live by the heart and stars up above
We'll drink with you till you fall down
We're the Pirates of Cookietown!"

concocting an album full of drinking and pirate songs with Lincoln. (Lincoln is more of a sounding board than a co-writer at this point.) The album is called *Milk and Beer: Laughing, Dancing, and Drinking Songs for Sons and Fathers*. It's a gift to Lincoln for his first birthday.

Much of this pirate material was inspired by Big Kenny's love of the Caribbean. Having vacationed there for years, he's developed a deep and abiding affection for sailing, the ocean, and the many salty characters down there whom he's befriended along the way. It's the pirate spirit—adventurous, carefree, and lustful—that he wants to pass along to his son with these songs.

The songs also involve drinking—in other words, something for Mom and Dad to relate to. One tune is called "I Heard We Had a Good

Time Last Night." Other titles include rousing chanteys like "The Pirates of Cookietown" and "Walk You Off the Plank." It's not hard to envision Lincoln and Big Kenny, in matching pirate outfits, marching around the living room, waving, respectively, a baby bottle and a beer bottle, and shouting out these ditties, and laughing "till the sun goes down."

DREAM ON

Big & Rich might last forever. Hell, we hope it does. We hope we're in our seventies and still writing songs and performing and leading the Freak Parade along an endless global journey. As mentioned earlier, John is the only guy that Big Kenny knows like John, and Big Kenny is the only guy John knows like Big Kenny. In some strange, perhaps unhealthy, way, we complement each other without either personality dominating the other. We are two alpha dogs who happen to get along instead of going for each other's throats. When you find something like that, and it works, it's hard to imagine that it's going to fall apart at any point in the future. It could happen, but it would be a shock—perhaps as big a shock as bumping into each other in the first place.

But if you asked either of us what we might be doing in ten or twenty years, either apart from or in addition to Big & Rich, we have some pretty definite answers.

VOTE JOHN RICH FOR PRESIDENT

If elected president of the United States in 2024, John will lower the drinking age to eighteen for all military personnel. If you are willing to die for this country, you've earned the right to have a beer. If you lose a comrade in battle, you should be allowed the right to toast them.

Big Kenny and Christiev on the road to their future.

As John tells virtually every interviewer when the question of the future comes up, he looks forward to the day when he becomes the president of the United States. He has already decided to run in the 2024 election, and would in fact be the first modern US president without a college education. He has an entire plan for doing this. This is not a joke. Big Kenny believes him. In fact, whenever it seems appropriate, Big Kenny will introduce John as the future president of the United States; John then emerges to the strains of "Hail to the Chief."

Here's the plan: Sometime in his forties, John plans to run for the governorship of his adopted home state, South Dakota. Politically, he sees himself as a passionate moderate, or maybe a purple-state Republican, slightly to the right of a blue-dog Democrat. More importantly, he wants to fashion himself after his political hero, Ronald Reagan. Whatever you think of his politics, Reagan had a backbone. He didn't put on an act of having a backbone, like a lot of spineless politicians tend to do. He actually had one.

Because of South Dakota's reputation as a swing state, John will fit right in. It's the perfect political soil for him to nurture a constituency that both agrees with him about Republican attitudes toward personal responsibility and small government, combined with a more Democratic take on protecting the environment and reaching out to help people in places as disparate as New Orleans and southern Sudan.

John loves South Dakota and would love nothing better than to use his notoriety to help the state grow and prosper and still maintain its pristine beauty. Plus, he sees himself as one of those citizen-politicians who isn't in it for the money or job security. By the time he's ready to run, he won't need the money or the fame or the pat on the back or all the perks that go along with being a high-profile politician.

As John sees it, a political leader whose only goal is to get in there and do what he thinks is best for the greatest number of people—well, that's a dangerous individual right there. And John fully plans to become that dangerous individual. He plans on putting out a tell-all book before he runs—no dirt to dig up for his opponent.

CODE NAME: ROXTAR

Since Big Kenny is a little older than John, he's not waiting for the future to arrive. He's making it happen right now. Assuming Big Kenny isn't appointed to a high cabinet position in the Rich administration—"Universal Ambassador of Love" would be appropriate—he will probably be out there trying to expand his own musical and entertainment horizons to a point—much like the vista where he and Christiev got married—that's as far as the eye can see.

On the drawing boards right now is a rock-opera theatrical film called *Code Name: Roxtar.* The story is simple: A country boy whose father is a failed songwriter moves from a small town to a big city and meets up with a group of musicians who share his dream of making it big in the music business. Via twelve original songs that vary widely in genre and style, the boy's ups and downs, both personal and professional, are chronicled until the dream finally comes true. He's on stage at the Grammys and the lights come up and there he is—rock star. Look for it soon in a theater or on a theatrical stage near you.

THE NEW ALBUM

At the same time we were working on this book, we were also working as hard as hell on the third Big & Rich album, which, like the others, we are co-writing and co-producing. It's hard to talk about something you're in the middle of creating. All we can say at this point is that after two albums and years on the road, we feel we've finally built the confidence and the will to take country music without prejudice even farther into uncharted territory—uncharted both musically and lyrically.

We now have a solid fan base. Maybe it took a little while to get the word out, but they're there now and they want us to take more risks and hopefully break a little new ground. For every person out there who goes, "You know, I don't get Big & Rich," there are now two, three, or four who reply, "Man, I do. I get them. Big time."

So we're not holding back. We're swinging for the fences. For example: We plan to include a country swing version of the AC/DC classic "You Shook Me All Night Long." Another anthem, called **"Radio,"** sounds like Big & Rich meets Def Leppard. It's huge, stadium-level country music.

On the other hand, there are songs that evoke something a little more otherworldly. One example is a new song called **"Eternity."** The idea behind it is that there is so much beauty in this life, it should be perfect here and now. Life should be so seamless that we don't know we've made it to the other side—eternity—until we in fact make it to the other side. Eternity, the song suggests, is

". . . more than a dream
Seems it's time I should move on but I hope you'll come with me
'Til I find eternity
Oh, baby, let's find eternity."

That's probably the best thing we can say about the new album right now. We're shooting for the sky. We're shooting for a kind of eternity.

OPPOSITE: Christiev and drummer Lincoln.

ABOVE: If Big & Rich were puppets.

Entertaining Big & Rich Style

✴

Both John and Big Kenny really know how to entertain their guests!

If you're ever invited to John's house, you might play some cards. His custom blackjack table is personalized with the names of the first four Godfathers of the Muzik Mafia: Godfather Big, Godfather Rich, Godfather Gierman, and Godfather Nicholson. They even have their own personalized deck of cards and set of chips!

Big Kenny might serve you a drink from his Pub of Luv bar, and then entertain you with a pirate tune. He even has the original sign from the Pub of Luv, which our good friend Mike Bowsher discovered in an antiques store in Nashville. The owner was reluctant to part with it, but being the car salesman that he is, Mike was able to liberate the historic sign from its temporary custodians. It currently hangs on the wall in Big Kenny's foyer above a black grand piano with his motto, LOVE EVERYBODY, painted on the side.

WHAT WE DO

BIG KENNY: "I've been broke a whole lot more than I've had anything in my life and I can tell you one thing—I've always been happy. Happiness is a state of mind, man, and it ain't a place and it ain't an amount in your bank account."

JOHN: "You know, we're so fortunate we live in a country where we get to make this music ... and we have to do it right ... that's the way I look at it every day. I go, *All right, what we're doing today—people are going to look back at this and judge us based on what we're doing today.*"

Frankly, it's a wonder that there was ever a Big & Rich in the first place.

Neither of us ever gave a thought of pairing up with another performer until it kind of happened in front of us. We were two solo artists, two hardheaded solo artists. We were like two dominant bulls in one herd, two I'm-running-this-show males in one pack. Neither of us was about to submerge our pretty hefty egos into one ego-less entity. If either of us was going to make it, it was on our own, singing our own unique brand of country or rock music.

But as the song **"Wild West Show"** says,

"There's never a hero in a battle of egos
There's never a winner in the quick draw."

When we first sat down to write songs together, we had to learn how to get along creatively, how to make it work for both of us simultaneously. That didn't happen overnight, but it happened. Nowadays we often find ourselves finishing each other's sentence or lyric. A good lyric is a good lyric, no matter whose mouth it came out of.

And the kind of "leave your ego at the door" attitude necessary to perform together on equal footing didn't happen overnight, either. But the longer we kept at it, the more sense it made. The longer we kept at it, the greater the realization that we were creating something much bigger than just the two of us put together. The whole was greater than the sum of its parts. It wasn't, as we said, one plus one equals two. It was one plus one equals ten.

One plus one equals a stage show—including Troy, Fred, the band, the fireworks, and our own performing fusion—that's way bigger than the two of us, and is sure to get even bigger. One plus one equals **"Save**

a Horse (Ride a Cowboy)," a much bigger party than either of us could have thrown on our own. One plus one equals **"8th of November,"** a simple song that led to a reawakening of our collective gratitude to Vietnam vets, not to mention a permanent memorial to the 173rd Airborne Brigade at Fort Benning. Could either of us have achieved something like that on our own? Fat chance.

It's a weird dynamic, that's for sure, but a dynamic that was forged in the early, crazy days of the Muzik Mafia. There were no rules about how performers interacted in the Mafia. If you were up there singing a new song by yourself and someone was moved to join you on stage and sing harmony, you didn't stop and say, "Hey, this is my song and you can't help me sing it." It was a jam session, and the whole idea was that something rich and powerful might occur if no prejudgment went on as to who could do what when. The next thing that popped into your head, unbeknownst to you or anyone else in the room, could be the best idea you ever had. Throw it out there and see if anyone responds.

The all-over-the-place music of Big & Rich is a direct result of the experience of those Tuesday nights where anything was possible musically. The Muzik Mafia was the research lab where together we proved that you could put pop singers, soul singers, bluegrass players, honky-tonkers, rappers, and rockers in the same room, and they could all get along and learn from one another. What would happen, when it all was working, was that the disparate styles of music would morph into something that didn't quite fit any of those convenient, preconceived labels. The old boundaries just didn't apply.

For the two of us, that small community of like-minded musicians and dreamers has now grown into a much larger community of fans, supporters, and comrades in arms. People like Niles Harris, Katie Darnell and all those working tirelessly toward a cure for cancer, the brave survivors of domestic violence willing to share their stories to help others, and the people fighting to stop the slaughter in Darfur. It's around interests like these that we came to realize that despite our differences in personal style or whatnot, something in addition to the love of music has bound us together and given us a common purpose and vision.

To put it bluntly, it's simply the desire to do good things.

Making music that gets people up and jumping around is obviously a good thing, and if you can do that, brother, then get out there and do it. But it doesn't stop there. We all have in us the capacity to do good things in the service of others, even great things. You don't have to have a title to do it. There is nothing that says that any of us, whatever place we come from in life—the backest of backwoods to the hoodiest of 'hoods—can't go forth and do great things. If it's in your heart, you can do it. You don't have to wait for someone to knight you and send you out.

Our particular mission, in our minds, is to break down the barriers that isolate us from one another and tend to breed fear, hatred, ignorance, and even death. The son of a preacher, John internalized at an early age the words of a common hymn:

"Red and yellow, black and white,
They are precious in his sight,
Jesus loves the little children of the world."

The goal is simple: blur the lines that artificially separate us. Music, properly understood, does this by its very nature. Listened to with an open mind, it's a common denominator of our shared humanity. The

end result, if we all sing along, so to speak, is simply a better place for all of us to live.

To quote John Lennon: "You may say I'm a dreamer / but I'm not the only one." And neither are we, not by a long shot.

Being able to freely express this, and damn near anything else that comes to mind, is one of the great things about living in this society and one of the reasons we want to keep reminding people in America not to take what we have for granted. We're preachers for good and we're patriots for America. That's who we are and what we do. We share, in John's term, the same evangelical DNA.

"Tell me brother, sisters, do you listen when it rains
Are you worried something's going to end it all today
Is there anything that you had wished that you had said
Or is it all just bouncing like a bubble in your head . . ."

That's from a song off our second record called **"Blow My Mind."** We figured from the beginning that if we were going to do this Big & Rich thing and do it right, we weren't going to do it half-ass. We weren't going to leave anything on the table and later regret that there was something we had wished to say and didn't. Musically, we weren't going to swallow our rock and pop urges to fit the country format, and we weren't going to swallow the lyrical opportunities of country to be more like those other formats. And we sure the hell weren't going to forgo the yin of loud and rowdy **"Comin' to Your City"** music for the yang of **"Holy Water."** We were going to do it all, man. We were going to do what moved us, and if people didn't like it, then no one would buy our records and we could go home and play them for the in-laws.

But that didn't happen, thank the Lord. The Freak Parade, God love you all, showed up at the party, kept it going well into the night, and continues to grow in both number and enthusiasm. As we mentioned before, we have only been doing this for four years. Thanks to your love and support, the Big & Rich express train is now tearing down the tracks going ninety miles an hour. The journey has just started.

John Rich, Big Kenny, Usher, Chad Kroeger, and Uncle Kracker at the Grammy Awards.

One more story. Growing up, one of the first jobs that Kenny had was logging—cutting trees down in the woods. He quickly came to see that the hardest place to fell a tree was in a healthy forest. The healthier the forest, the stronger all the trees were that grew up together. They supported and protected one another. If a tree should get knocked over in a storm, the other trees were there to hold it up until it could regain its stature.

It's easy to see how that analogy carries over to the whole Big & Rich experience. If you decide to go through the world alone, you're asking for trouble. When you stumble, which you surely will, you're liable to fall on your face. When you surround yourself with friends, though, you might fall over but you won't fall down. A forest of friends will get you through damn near anything. It's for good reason that every day we thank God for all the wonderful friends, from Two Foot Fred to Six Foot Troy and everyone in between, who have helped us keep standing.

Music without prejudice. Creativity without bureaucracy. All genres welcome. Musically Artistic Friends in Alliance. World domination!

Hey, that's what we're working on here, and thanks to all of you out there for putting up with us.

Big Kenny & John Rich

These two guitars
are now displayed
in the Country
Music Hall of Fame
in Nashville,
Tennessee.

We'll see you later. Bye bye, now.

Bye bye. Too-da-loo.

See ya.

Adiós.

So long, y'all.

Close the book.

Or start it over.

PHOTO CREDITS

✳

Bill Alphin: 2 (right), 3 (top)

Christiev Alphin: 55, 184 (bottom), 206–207

Kristin Barlowe: xx (bottom), xxiv, 19, 23, 202, 203, 204, 212, 214

David Bean: 35

Joan Bush: 170 (top)

Matt Chang: ii (bottom), 51 (right), 74, 111, 116, 140

Gary Chapman: 16, 196

Tom Donoghue: 158, 160–161

Cory Gierman: 11, 22, 30, 38

Tom Griffith: ii (top left)

Joe Hardick: x, xiv, 5 (top left), 6 (bottom), 13, 26, 45, 88 (top), 104, 106, 108, 121 (bottom), 125, 128, 132, 135, 136, 142, 144, 145, 162, 166–167, 172, 173, 175, 177, 178–179, 180, 183, 188, 192–193, 197, 205, 209 (bottom), 228–229

Sheila Hozhabri: xiii, 7 (middle), 7 (bottom), 25, 29, 31, 49, 54, 64, 65, 99 (right), 101, 109, 112, 117, 131, 146, 153, 186 (bottom), 190, 191, 194, 201, 211, 215, 216, 217, 230

Curt Jenkins: vi, xx (top), 107, 110 (top), 141

Judy Jenkins: viii, 120 (top)

Jesse Josleyn: 123

Big Kenny: 3 (bottom)

Marc Oswald: ii (top middle), iii, iv, xviii–xix, xxii, 2 (left), 7 (top), 8, 10, 17, 18, 20, 21, 24, 28, 32, 39, 42–43, 47, 48, 52, 57, 59, 60–61, 63, 66, 69, 70, 76, 77, 78, 80, 81, 82, 84–85, 86, 87, 88 (bottom), 89, 91, 92, 94, 95, 96, 97, 98, 99 (left), 100, 102 (bottom left), 102 (top right), 102 (bottom right), 102 (middle right), 102 (middle left), 103, 103 (middle), 103 (top), 110 (bottom), 113, 122, 126–127, 139, 150, 163, 164, 165, 170 (bottom), 184 (top), 186 (top), 199, 208, 209 (top), 218, 220, 221, 223

Gavin Peters: 41

Rachel Kice: 51 (left)

Shawn Pennington: 44, 102 (top left), 115, 118–119, 121 (top), 224–225

Jim Rich: 5 (top right), 6 (top), 195

Warner Bros. Nashville: 46, 58, 93, 94 (bottom), 154

Jules Wortman: xxi

AVAILABLE NOW
THE NEW ALBUM FROM

Big & Rich

BETWEEN RAISING HELL
AND AMAZING GRACE

WBRNASHVILLE.COM BIGANDRICH.COM